PRAYER
CAN
CHANGE
YOUR
MARRIAGE

PRAYER
CAN
CHANGE
YOUR
MARRIAGE

by
Ron Auch

New Leaf Press

First printing, 1985
Second printing, November 1990
Third printing, July 1992
Fourth printing, May 1996

Copyright © 1984, 1990 by New Leaf Press, Inc. All rights reserved. Printed in the United States of America. No part of this book may be used or reproduced in any manner whatsoever without written permission of the publisher, except in the case of brief quotations in articles and reviews. For information write New Leaf Press, Inc., P.O. Box 726, Green Forest, AR 72638.

ISBN: 0-89221-118-0
Library of Congress: 84-61916

Scripture quotations are from the New American Standard Bible.

DEDICATION

To my most precious wife, Lou Ann. If it were not for her ability to put up with me, we would never have come this far.

CONTENTS

INTRODUCTION

Like never before, marriages in the Church are failing. Divorce, at one time shocking, is now common place among believers. Increasingly, couples with marital problems are considering divorce a realistic option.

The Church has responded with good intentions, but with very little else. Marriage seminars are offered, but they usually seem to address the symptoms and not the problems. Husbands are urged to do thoughtful things to make their wives feel special, such as bringing them flowers. Wives are counseled to work hard to be the perfect housewife, the quintessential June Cleaver, welcoming their husbands home with an elegant dinner and beautiful home. The divorce statistics continue to climb.

Very few preachers and teachers seem convinced that the problem married couples are facing is a spiritual one. After experiencing difficulties in my marriage, I know that it is. And I know that bouquets of flowers and elegant dinners are not solutions because they touch only the surface of the marriage, not the cores of the individuals where the real troubles reside. But I also know there is only one way to restore marriages, and that is through prayer. It changed my marriage, and prayer can change your marriage.

CHAPTER ONE

TESTIMONY

"Behold, the Old Things Have Passed Away—But They Don't Always Stay That Way"

It was a warm, lazy summer afternoon when a neighborhood friend called me on the phone and told me he had something really neat to show me at his house. Like any twelve year old boy, I was curious and went to his house to investigate. When I got there, he met me at the door with a peculiar grin and invited me in. I still wasn't sure what it was he wanted to show me, but evidently it was something secret because he closed and locked his bedroom door behind us. He disappeared under his bed and reappeared with a handful of magazines. They weren't *Sports Illustrated, Hot Rod,* or *Mad* magazines, the ones that had been popular with my friends and me. However, their titles were familiar; everybody heard of *Playboy* and *Penthouse,* even me. As we studied each page, I couldn't believe my eyes and the effect it had on me. It uncovered drives and feelings in me that I didn't know existed. When I left my friend's house that day, I felt like a different person, and in many ways I was. The subsequent weeks and months proved it. I quickly found myself hooked on pornography.

My family's religion didn't inhibit me from indulging myself in my dark new interests. That was probably true because my family wasn't really a Christian family, although we were very close to each other and attended a nice Lutheran church. But as far as religion went, that was all we did: attended services. We basically just did our religious duty every week and then went home without really being effected. It wasn't anything personal, and it seemed rather irrelevant to my life. Certainly I was confirmed when the time came. That's what was expected of you when you were in the ninth grade, so I complied. I looked upon it as my graduation from church. I recited the vows I was trained to recite, but when confirmation classes ended, so did my church attendance.

Like any boy entering high school, I thought a lot about girls. I mean real girls, the kind I could go out with and have a relationship with, not just the female objects in my pornography. For the most part, however, thinking about them was the extent of my involvement with them. I was short and overweight, and those just weren't the qualities girls were looking for in guys. My older brother Doug, on the other hand, was the exact opposite. He was tall, slim, and really quite handsome so he had all the girls chasing after him (and yes, at times it did seem like **all** the girls were chasing after him). That made me feel even worse about myself. I remember lamenting, "Doug, I'll never have the girls chase me the way they chase you." He just shrugged off my self-doubt and replied matter-of-factly, "Ron, all you have to do is work out, lose weight, and they'll come running." But I couldn't lose weight, and they didn't come running. They didn't even come trickling. It wasn't long until I convinced myself that no girl would ever like me and I would be a lifelong bachelor.

My fixation with pornography began to influence my life greatly. As I look back on those days, I am repulsed by critics who say pornography has little real effect on young people. I experienced the destructive effects of pornography for years, and it very nearly destroyed my life.

My Family's Damascus Road

While I was in high school, Doug got married. This came as no surprise to me. I always knew my brother would get married. Tina, the girl he married, grew up in a born-again Christian family, but she wasn't living for the Lord at the time, and, therefore, she had no compunctions about marrying my non-Christian brother. Not too many years after they got married, things began to go sour between them. The fact of that matter is they were just plain miserable. Out of sheer desperation, Tina rededicated her life to Christ. The change in her disposition astonished my brother. Her phenomenal transformation impressed him so deeply that he, too, dedicated his life to Jesus and was born again. Their marriage was just as transformed as they were individually, and it still stands strong today.

Almost immediately, Doug and Tina enlisted the believers at their church to pray for my family and me. The consistency of their prayers paid off; four years later, my parents and I went down to the altar to give our lives to Christ. My brother, Barry, followed in our footsteps a week later. Having the entire family saved was exciting, especially because my brothers and I were mechanics at my dad's garage. We told our customers about Jesus at every opportunity. We even turned our garage into a Christian garage. (You do that by taking down the old calendars and replacing them with new ones.)

For a couple of months, everything was wonderful. It was a brand new life with a brand new perspective. The old things had passed away, and all things were made new. But then one day while I was in a drug store, I paused at a magazine rack for what was supposed to be only a second. That second turned into several minutes spent leafing through porn magazines. That incident devastated me. It seemed as if all those terrible things I had thought were dead were being resurrected. I was hooked all over again.

Perhaps the worst part about the ordeal was my feeling of absolute aloneness. First of all, I was sure that I was the only born-again Christian with this problem. Secondly, because of my immaturity in the things of God, I figured that if I talked to my pastor about it, he wouldn't understand. I thought he would be thoroughly mortified and would ask me to stop attending his church before I contaminated anyone else with my depravity. Satan had deceived me into believing that I was trapped in a catch-twenty-two situation: I was having little or no luck trying to kick my habit alone, and I couldn't go to anyone more mature in the Lord because I thought I would totally scandalize and alienate them.

Trying to Kick the Habit

In spite of my old struggles with pornography, I sensed God's call on my life to be a minister. As I prepared to leave for North Central Bible College in Minneapolis, Minnesota, I determined that I would shake my problem. I was moving away to a new place. I was going to Bible college where I would concentrate on God and on God alone. With this new beginning, I was determined to start a new life, free of those old bondages. However, my new life died a quick death, lasting barely a couple days. My problems persisted. The big city offered even more opportunities to indulge my flesh, and the more I yielded to them, the guiltier I felt. In fact, it was even worse than being back home because I was at Bible college, where I had far greater expectations for myself. There I was, studying to be a minister of the gospel! How could I be simultaneously struggling with pornography? After some consideration, I rationalized that my problem was that I needed to get married. Marriage would give me an honorable, godly outlet for my feelings, I reasoned.

During my first summer in Minneaplis, I met the girl who was to be my wife, in church. One Sunday morning after service, a friend of mine directed my attention to a group of girls. "Do you see the dark-haired one?" he continued. I grinned at him and answered, "Not only do I see her now, but I have had my eye on her for some time." My friend nodded slowly. "I can't blame you," he said. "She's the only one in the lot of them that would make a good wife." That settled it for me. I had to at least try to get to know her. And I did. We fell in love with each other, and one year later, we were married. With this new beginning, I was determined to start a new life, free of those old bondages (again). However, my new life died a quick death (again), lasting just a couple weeks, and my problems persisted. In point of fact, they grew even worse.

If I learned anything, it was that marriage, like going to Bible college, does not solve problems. It intensifies them. All I succeeded in doing was bringing my lustful spirit into our marriage. My self-seeking, self-serving spirit of lust crushed her gentle, sweet spirit. As a result, she was repulsed by me and not drawn to me physically in the least. Within six months, our honeymoon was over and with it our sex life. What I thought would satisfy my fleshly drive actually intensified it.

To put it mildly, we were at an impasse. Yet, I never took it out on her. In my heart, I knew I was at fault. I knew that the problem was in me. At that time in my life when I needed prayer most, my prayer life was nominal at best. I prayed periodically. I prayed on Sundays. I prayed if someone asked me to pray for them. What I lacked in my life was a well-developed prayer habit.

Entering the Ministry—and More Problems

One year after we were married, we were in the ministry. Although I was still attending Bible college, for the last two years of my education I served full time in a church in South St. Paul, Minnesota. By that time, my problems seemed to be snowballing. Not only had this problem with lust gone unchecked in me as a new Christian, it had continued in me as a Bible college student, and then as a minister. I staggered beneath the ponderous weight of failure. I had failed to overcome it as a student at Bible college. Worst of all, I was also failing as a minister. To make matters worse, my wife was rejecting my advances toward her. This just intensified my need for more pornography.

Lou Ann and I still tried to work out our marital problems, but we couldn't even seem to clearly identify what those problems were. I felt that our problems were a result of the intimacy our marriage lacked. So whenever we discussed our problems, I always directed the discussion back to our lack of intimacy. This, in turn, would frustrate Lou Ann and she would inevitably reply, "All you ever talk about is sex. Is that all you're interested in?"

In all honesty, for a period of about four years, all we did about sex was talk, and we didn't even do much of that. During that period, we never laid a hand on each other. Occasionally, there were hugs and kisses, but nothing more. During that period, I discovered that "R"-rated movies tended to be sexually explicit and not socially frowned upon. Living in a large metropolitan area, I found many movie theaters that were open during the afternoon, and I ended up sneaking off to see these movies every week. I continued to feel guilty, but tried to console myself with the fact that the movies were not as explicit as the magazines had been. But my guilt and anguish still intensified because I was an associate pastor at the time, and I recalled that to him whom much is given, much is required.

I was faced with a drive that I couldn't control. Today, many young men have the same drive, but it has become an acceptable thing for Christians to attend even "R"-rated movies. Christians who do such things are making terrible mistakes. First, they don't realize that what they are doing hurts God. Second, they fail to realize that what they see in the movies is a fantasy. As they try to implement what they see on the big screen in their marriages, they don't get Hollywood's happy ending. All they get is the cold harsh reality of the consequences of their actions: broken relationships, sexually transmitted diseases, and so on. Third, and most tragically, their lustful spirits will crush their wives' spirits. Clearly, marriage does not solve problems. It only compounds them. Our commitment to Christ is the only thing that solves problems.

Steps in the Right Direction

I had already tried many things to alleviate my problems, but I wasn't ready to give up. I decided that perhaps working for my Master's Degree would help, so we moved to Kenosha, a city in southeastern Wisconsin situated between Milwaukee and Chicago. The seminary I wanted to attend, Trinity Evangelical Divinity, was located in nearby Deerfield, Illinois. Everything seemed to be coming together. I was convinced that this was the beginning of my new life without my lust problem. But like my other new beginnings, this one failed to alleviate my problem. Within two weeks, I was driving to Milwaukee and Chicago where I could see movies without risking getting caught.

A gray blanket of depression descended upon me. Up until that point, I had been able to hide behind a smile which prevented anyone from suspecting that anything was the matter. But I was fast becoming overwhelmed by despair. Deep down inside, I knew I was not the husband I was supposed to be, and I was not the Christian I was supposed to be. In addition, our family was not developing at all. Occasionally my wife would discuss having a child, but when I would remind her of the intimacy that would be required, such discussions would end abruptly. Our need for intimacy never seemed to click with my wife. We had been married for six years, and we still didn't have any children. As we were both reaching our upper twenties, I felt that our time for having children was running short.

Starting a New Life—Really

Just after we moved to Kenosha, the church we joined was promoting a seminar which was going to be held there in a couple weeks. An evangelist named Dick Eastman was going to be teaching about prayer for a week. For some reason, an enthusiasm built within me as the seminar dates neared. I actually felt confident—like never before—that I was about to find the thing I needed to straighten myself out.

I had tried just about everything else. Somehow prayer had to be the solution.

I wasn't disappointed. Dick's teaching touched me deeply. I don't mean that his teachings just made me feel there was hope for me. They did that, but there was more. I began giving myself to God in prayer. I gave up trying to solve my problems myself. It dawned on me that I had really been approaching my life and ministry backwards. I was seeking all kinds of answers to my problems, but I was never seeking God. Then it hit me. God is the answer! I hadn't realized this before because I had been using prayer almost exclusively to ask God to take care of my problems. I hadn't been seeking God at all, just a solution to my problem.

Finally, during that prayer seminar, I realized this. Steadily I developed a craving in my heart for God. I wanted to experience Romans 8:26 which states: "The spirit knows how to help us because we don't know how to pray as we should. But our groanings are too great for words." I wanted a desire for God that was so great that I would feel as if my chest were going to explode, that I could do no more than groan out my feelings to God. Eventually, that is exactly what happened. I would spend the first hour or more just saying, "Oh, God, Oh, God." Soon it would come from deep within, and I would begin to groan out my feelings. For the first time in my life, I began to experience what I really needed. I didn't need all the pornography. I needed God. During all those years of asking God for help with my problem, God was trying to say to me, "Ron, what you need is Me!" God became my new pursuit and obsession.

Even with that, nothing really changed physically in our marriage. Prayer ultimately was the catalyst for the renovation of my marriage, but the changes didn't occur right away. The great changes I anticipated hadn't materialized nearly as quickly as I had figured. I was the one who had been having a problem, my wife wasn't. Her attitude was, "We're fine. Our marriage is working. So what if there's no intimacy?" Certainly, we had a lot of things going for us maritally. I had no doubt that Lou Ann loved me. She expressed her love to me in many ways. We were also working successfully in our youth ministry and having a lot of fun doing so. In the midst of all that, I was being eaten away inside by guilt. I knew my wife had no desire for me because of my secret life of lust.

I remember being in a motel room with my wife during this period of our marriage. We were both lying on the bed. I looked at her, and in my heart I said, "God, when will You give me my wife?" Immediately, God spoke to my heart and said, "Just as soon as you give Me yourself." Through prayer, an awareness of God began to permeate my life. My love for God began to change. I began to pray for God's sake and not for mine. I found myself praying not just to see what I could get, but because God needs someone to pray and because of what I felt God wanted to do through my prayers for His kingdom. My love for God became so strong that I started to refrain from lustful thoughts simply because I didn't want to hurt God. At the same time, I didn't want to hurt myself, and every time I sinned, my growth with Him slowed down. Before this, I had avoided sin mostly out of a desire for self-aggrandizement. I figured, "If I can get over this lust problem, my marriage will be better, and then I will be fulfilled." Now my predominant motivation for and strength in overcoming sin is my love for God which has grown through spending time in His presence.

This doesn't infer perfection. I wasn't immediately delivered from my problem. Nonetheless, God accepted me into His presence and forgave my sins. In fact, my greatest times in prayer were on the days when I had great sins to confess. This is because God's grace is greatest when we are at our most unworthy point. If we were worthy, grace would have no value to us. It is our sinfulness that gives grace its merit. Moreover, not only was I accepted into God's presence, but I found that God was strengthening my resistance to temptation. My resistance was usually directly proportional to the amount of time I spent in prayer.

An important lesson in that trying point of our marriage was that I did not blame my wife. That prevented us from having serious arguments and probably prevented our marriage from dissolving. Every once in a while, I would try to put the blame on her by telling her she wasn't living up to the Scripture which says we own each other's bodies, but for the most part, I realized I was to blame for our problems.

God is not concerned about blame. Determining blame will not solve a problem. God is simply looking for someone who will submit his or her will to Him. He wants only to get us to seek Him so that He can bring about the changes that are needed. God can work just as effectively through the guilty person as He can through the innocent one. By letting God work in me, He has given me my heart's desire through my wife.

Although results were not immediate, they did come. Two years after I started to pray, Lou Ann and I spent some days together camping. It was a beautiful time of relaxing, fishing, and playing table games. I believe the Holy Spirit used that time together to complete the healing that was necessary for our marriage. Shortly after that, Lou Ann and I experienced something closely akin to a second honeymoon. It was a beautiful time of getting to know each other again. Finally, nine years after we were married, our son, Ronnie, Jr. was born.

CHAPTER TWO

Why Should We Worship God?

*They that worship God merely from fear would worship
the devil, too, if he appear.*
—Thomas Fuller,
Ghomologia, no. 6419

My new life of prayer brought me closer to God than I
ever though possible, but there was still a lot of spiritual
growing ahead of me. One of the areas I needed growth in
most was worship. I participated in worship regularly, both
in public and in private. However, I began to discover that my
reasons for worshiping were amiss. I worshiped God for
what He had done and in anticipation of what I hoped He
would do for me, but I never worshiped God simply because
of who He is.

The greatest cause for worshiping God we can have is
just that fact that He is who He is. If God never answered
another one of our prayers for the rest of our lives, He would
still be worthy of our worship because of who He is. When I
worship God, I express my love to Him and I praise Him for

who He is. I tell Him how much I need, want, and desire Him. Worship has become the most intimate part of my prayer life and the part I look forward to most.

Worshiping God for the Things He Can Give Us?

When I am at home, I have a special place where I pray, and I am very comfortable there. When I am traveling in my capacity as an evangelist, though, I don't have the luxury of that special place. Sometimes I end up in a place that is just not conducive to prayer at all. I remember one Sunday when I was staying at the home of a family that attended the church where I was ministering. I had risen early to pray in the bedroom they had given me, but after I was praying for a short time, the family rose and began to get ready for church. They did nothing out of the ordinary, but it was very distracting for me. I finally decided to postpone my prayer time until later in the day.

While I was in church that day, I began to experience something I had never experienced before. I wanted desperately to get away and be alone with God. I had been a Christian for many years by this time, but I never really longed to spend time with God like that. I was practically drumming my fingers on my Bible, waiting for the service to end so that I could go spend time with God. Then the irony of the situation struck me. I was in what that church called their worship service, and I really couldn't sense anything. I didn't sense the presence of God in that place as I did when I worshiped God alone or even at different churches. I noticed that very few people were worshiping God. Many were just looking around to see who else was in church, others were just mouthing the words to songs whose meanings were long forgotten. I began to feel the longing in God's heart for His people to worship Him. A few days later, as I was reading the book of Ezekiel, that incident came to mind.

And they come to you as people come, and they sit before you as My people, and hear your words, but they do not do them, for they do the lustful desires expressed by their mouth, and their heart goes after their gain (Ezk. 33:31).

That verse describes an average church service. People today are often sitting before God as His people, but the only love they show God is a love for what God can give them. Worse yet, this is being condoned and even sanctioned from many pulpits. Many preachers have elevated materialism and avarice to the status of theology by vigorously admonishing their listeners to go out and possess all the material wealth they can because they are the "King's kids." They tell congregations that because they are children of God, they deserve the best. I have no quarrel with that because God only gives the best. But what do we want God's best for? Do we want it simply to fulfill our own lust and covetousness, or do we want it so we can further the kingdom of God? This question is seldom raised, and these preachers have little to say about worshiping God for who He is. That is the greatest problem; not that one seeks to fulfill his "God-given rights," but that he does so without really seeking God. Sadly, these proprietors of what I call sanctified materialism preach all about our rights as the "King's kids" without knowing very much about the King. If they knew more about Him, they would not distract attention from Jesus to the things Jesus can procure for us. If they knew more about Him, they would know that such unbridled selfishness breaks His heart.

A very basic error that Christians make today is assuming that material prosperity is a sure sign of God's favor. This is not the case. God has established certain divine principles which govern the acquisition of wealth. For example, "Give and it will be given unto you...." God will honor that principle regardless of who practices it. If a pagan practices that principle, he will find God staying true to His Word because His Word never returns to Him void. God honoring His Word doesn't necessarily enhance the love relationship between Him and the one who puts His principles into practice. We can see the same thing happening between the parents who promise their child he can have any toy he wants if he gets "A"s in all his classes. If their child does it, they will fulfill their obligation by buying him any toy he wants, but it doesn't necessarily enhance the love between them. It is nothing more than the fulfillment of an agreement. That's not nearly enough to base a relationship on. Imagine if your relationship with your child was limited to his wants and whims for new toys in exchange for his good grades. Imagine asking him to go to the park or to the zoo with you because you just wanted to spend time with him. Then imagine him turning down your offer because he wanted to go to the toy store to pick out his next new toy. You'd be bound by your word to him, new toys for his grades, but you would have a very cold and empty relationship in which your child no longer desired your company or your love—just your gifts.

Many people say they want God or that they want to worship God. But why? Peter Lord once remarked, "Do you want God, so you can use God to fulfill your own ends, or do you want God, so God can use you to fulfill His own ends?" There is a world of difference between the two. If you want the former, you really don't want God. What you really want is a genie who will obediently grant your every wish. It is a master-servant relationship with you as the master. If on the other hand, you seek the latter, you are indeed seeking God. To an extent, this implies a master-servant relationship, too, but in this one, God is the master and you are the servant.

Diligently Seeking God

Shortly after I began praying, "God, I don't want anything else; I just want You," I began to realize the cost of having that prayer answered. I sensed God speaking to my heart, saying, "If you really want Me, you are going to have to give up your love for things." Until that moment, I didn't realize just how attached I was to many of the things in my life, perhaps even more attached than I was to Him. As I opened myself to Him, God began stripping away my love for things. This didn't mean I had to part with the things themselves, just with my love for those things. I learned that Christians can possess many things, and there is nothing wrong with that. It's when things possess the Christian that he's in trouble.

As I continued to diligently seek God, worship became a greater priority in my prayer time. Worship brought me into a greater awareness of the ever abiding presence of God, and that was what I wanted. God inhabits the praises of His people, and if I'm really going to seek God relentlessly, then my tendency will be to practice those things which increase my sensitivity of His presence. When God is my objective, when God is the reason I pray, I will spend much time simply worshiping Him. However, if things are my objective in prayer, I won't spend much time worshiping God but rather, worshiping what worship can get me: things from God. There is a tendency today to worship the act of worship rather than God.

Two Kinds of Seekers

I once heard Peter Lord speak about two kinds of seekers. The first kind is the beggar. When I lived in Minneapolis, I would occasionally be approached by beggars. They always looked at my hands, seldom ever looking me straight in the eyes. That's because they were looking to see what my hands were going to take out of my pockets for them. Basically, all the beggar is seeking is what he can get out of someone materially, so he looks to the hands.

The second kind of seeker is the lover. Unlike the beggar, the lover looks to the eyes. The lover is looking for love in return, and that love can be perceived in the eyes. When I was dating my wife, I could drop her off in front of her dormitory after a date and she could give me a look that would set me off for a whole week. That look told me that she loved me. When you are in love, what you need more than anything else is to know that the one whom you are seeking love from approves of you, so you look to the eyes. Throughout His written Word, God is saying, "You who love Me, seek My face." Yet today, many Christians persist in seeking only His hand.

I became a lover of my wife and of my God. I didn't seek my wife just to see what I could get out of her materially. I sought her, not the things she possessed. It taught me a great lesson about the kingdom of God. Even though I went after my wife's eyes, I ended up with her hand in marriage. The hand represents material things. In other words, once you've got God, you have all that He possesses. Scripture tells us that if we "seek first His kingdom and His righteousness; and all these things shall be added to you" (Matt. 6:33). If we seek God, He will provide the things we have need of. I don't need to seek things from God because those things come automatically as a result of getting God. God has done more for me materially since I started going after Him than He ever did when I was just seeking things. In praying for your marriage, you must make this a priority. You must want God more than a good marriage. Make God your pursuit and the end result will be a happy home.

CHAPTER THREE

Fruit For God

Therefore, my brethren, you also were made to die to the Law through the body of Christ...that we might bear fruit for God. For while we were in the flesh, the sinful passions, which were aroused by the Law, were at work in the members of our body to bear fruit for death (Rom. 7:4,5).
—Paul the apostle

Like trees, we all bear fruit, but like trees, we do not necessarily bear good fruit. As Christians, we have the option of bearing either fruit for God or fruit for death. If one bears fruit for God, the Lord will use it to draw one's spouse and children to Him. Jesus came to bring us life and that more abundantly, and His is the kind of fruit God can use to build His kingdom. Fruit for death, the other kind of fruit, runs contrary to God's kingdom. It breeds and perpetuates final, absolute, spiritual death. Yet in one important way, we are not like trees: we have the ability to choose what kind of fruit we will bear.

For the flesh sets its desire against the Spirit, and the Spirit against the flesh; for these are in opposition to one

*another, so that you may not do the things that you
please (Gal. 5:17).*

In this passage from his letter to the Galatians, Paul
explains exactly how it is we are able to choose what kind of
fruit we will bear. He makes it clear that in the heart of every
man, a struggle rages between the flesh and the Spirit. They
are diametrically opposed to each other. Neither of them
wants to do what the other wants to do. Consequently a fierce
contest between them ensues. If the flesh conquers the Spirit,
fruit for death will be produced. If the Spirit emerges victorious, fruit for God will be produced. It is because we can
decide whether the Spirit or the flesh wins out that we can
determine which kind of fruit we will bear. Quite simply, the
one we give into the most determines the type of fruit our
lives produce. Prayer is an excellent example of this struggle.
If we cannot deny the flesh for the purpose of seeking God,
the flesh will come to dominate us. Living according to the
dictates of the flesh leads one inevitably to produce fruit for
death. If, on the other hand, we deny the flesh and relentlessly
seek God, the Spirit will dominate. Living according to the
Spirit leads one inevitably to produce fruit for God.

Paul also describes in detail what fruit for death is:

*Now the deeds of the flesh are evident, which are: immor-
ality, impurity, sensuality, idolatry, sorcery, enmities,
strife, jealousy, outbursts of anger, disputes, dissen-
sions, factions, envyings, drunkenness, carousings...
(Gal. 5:19-21).*

These are the types of things your life will produce if you
cannot say "No" to the desires of your flesh. These things will
entrench themselves in your life if you do not deny the flesh.
If you continually give in to your flesh, there is absolutely no
way to avoid bearing bad fruit. The only way to circumvent
fruit for death, is by denying the flesh and living according to
the Spirit. Paul is equally clear about the fruit that living for
the Spirit produces.

But the fruit of the Spirit is love, joy, peace, patience, kindness, goodness, faithfulness, gentleness, self-control... (Gal. 5:22,23).

This is the fruit of God. It is cultivated in the life of one who denies the flesh and lives according to the Spirit. This kind of individual allows the Spirit of God to drive him into godly habits like prayer, studying the Bible, and telling those around them about Jesus. The fruit that springs from this person's life is the type that God can use to draw others to Christ.

Parable of the Vineyard

Isaiah's parable of the vineyard provides us with further insight into fruit bearing (Isa. 5:1-7). Verse 1 begins, "Let me sing now for my well-beloved a song of my beloved concerning His vineyard. My well-beloved had a vineyard on a fertile hill." Isaiah started his parable by telling us about God's vineyard, symbolic of God's people. He explained that God placed His vineyard on a hill where the soil was fertile. In other words, God has placed each one of us in a place where we could produce something of value to Him. No man will be justified when he stands before God and tries to explain that he did nothing for God because of his circumstances. We often try to use our circumstances as a justification for doing nothing for God. We say things like, "I can't serve God because of my mate," or "I can't get anything done for God until He gets me a new car." However, according to Isaiah, God has planted everyone of us where the soil is fertile. It is good soil, it can produce.

In verse 2 we read, "And He dug it all around, removed its stones, and planted it with the choicest vine. And He built a tower in the middle of it...." In this verse, we see the whole process of salvation. First, it talks about digging around the vineyard. Some of the translations read, "He placed a fence around it." Either way, it mentions a protective hedge around the vineyard. Interestingly enough, this protection is there even before the stones, symbolic of our sins, are removed.

In Bible college, I attended a class called Systematic Theology. For a period of time, we discussed something called prevenient grace. Prevenient grace is the grace of God that is at work in our lives even before salvation. The word prevenient simply means, "that which goes before." Jesus said, "No one comes unto the Father but by Me." Therefore whether we recognized it or not, Jesus was at work in our lives long before we came to a place of salvation. Many times that work of prevenient grace could have come in a protective measure, a hedge of protection. I can think back to the days before I knew Christ, and today I recognize God was protecting me long before I came to Christ.

After that protective hedge was established, Isaiah reported that the stones were removed. This is representative of the salvation experience in which one's sins are removed. Stones in the vineyard would hinder growth, just as sin in our lives also hinders growth. Then He planted the choicest vine. In other words, God has given us the best seed He could find: the Word of God. There is no greater seed than God's Word. Isaiah himself referred to God's Word as a seed in Chapter 55 of his book. So God has implanted us with His Word. Next in the parable, he built a tower. The tower is symbolic of the Holy Spirit. The tower offers protection because it acts as a warning of impending danger.

So to this point we find that God has drawn us to Himself, has removed our sins (stones), has given us His Word (seed), and has given us His Holy Spirit (tower). Then we find that He has built a wine press, symbolic of pressure, in the middle of the vineyard. Under pressure, God finds out what kind of fruit we, symbolized by the vineyard, are producing. In fact, pressure may be the only means of testing our fruit, symbolized by the grapes in the vineyard. You can put a grape in your mouth and roll it around all day, but you'll never know if it is a good grape or a sour grape. The only way to determine its quality is by applying pressure and biting down on it. If under pressure you come forth with anger, vengeance, and hatred, you demonstrate that your fruit is fruit for death. If, however, under pressure, you come forth with love, joy, and peace, you reveal a harvest of fruit for God.

Producing fruit figures very prominently into God's plan for each of us. God wants to use the fruit of our lives to minister to those around us, especially to those who put the most pressure on us. In so doing, the fruit from our lives can actually minister to the shortcomings of those people. It must be understood first that we pressure others and others pressure us because of the lack of God's character. If my fictional co-worker, Oscar, lacks kindness, that lack will ultimately put pressure on me. But if I can respond to that pressure with kindness, God can use what my life is producing to meet the need in Oscar's life. That is fruit for God. If, however, under pressure I can't respond with kindness and I retaliate, then I have produced fruit for death. In that unhappy event, my life is producing fruit that is actually killing the work of God in Oscar's life.

Opposites

Did you ever wonder why opposites attract? I'm sure we've all heard about two people who are sure they're in love and, consequently, get married. Then after a couple months, they look at each other and ask, "Why in the world did we get married? We are complete opposites!" It happens quite frequently, but it doesn't imply that one partner is inferior to the other or that one is all good or all bad. When you consider opposites, you are dealing with two people who both have strengths and weaknesses. Often one person's strengths attracted the other person's weaknesses. Perhaps this is because weakness cannot resist strength. My weaknesses were naturally drawn to my wife's strengths. At the same time her weaknesses were drawn to my strengths. That seems to simplify the mystery of why opposites attract, and even seems to promise that they always will. But complications can arise from this.

For example, the flesh cannot stand weakness. Strength has no compassion on weakness. Therefore, even though my weakness was drawn to my wife's strength, her flesh in the natural was repelled by my weakness. Most of us are that way. However, we must not react the way the flesh would like us to. That would produce fruit for death. We must react the way the Spirit of God in us wants us to, with compassion and empathy for the weaknesses of others. That is fruit for God.

A Bad Harvest

The last part of verse 2 tells us, "...Then He expected it to produce good grapes, but it produced only worthless ones." God had constructed the best vineyard under the best conditions. He gave it every opportunity for success, provided it with everything it needed to produce a bumper crop of the best produce. Yet all He found were bad grapes. How could that be? Verse 3 then challenges us to judge between God and His vineyard to determine whose fault it was that only bad grapes had been produced.

"What more was there to do for My vineyard that I have not done in it?" God asked in verse 4. God is saying that He has done absolutely everything necessary in our lives to enable us to be effective for Him. Specifically, He died on the cross for our sins. That is the greatest and most monumental thing He could do for us. In that regard, we have all been partakers equally. No one has more salvation than anyone else. Everyone has received the same forgiveness of sin, the same Word of God, and the same Holy Spirit. In the end, God judges our effectiveness for Him based on what He did once and for all equally at Calvary.

Believers seem preoccupied with contriving and collecting excuses to explain why they can't serve God. The greatest reason it is so difficult to get people to do anything for God is because of the day we live in. Paul talked about this in his second letter to Timothy, warning that in the last days, an Apostate Church would rise. He predicted that the Apostate Church would be marked by the Apostate believer. Such a believer would be a man that knows God (in our vernacular, we would say he is born again), but who would not allow the truth that he knows to prompt him to any service for God. In essence, Paul said that in the last days, the church will be full of people that know God but refuse to do anything for Him. It will be a day of backyard barbecues and high-speed boats, but no service for God.

Then in verse 5 of Isaiah 5, we find everything that happened in verse 2 is being reversed. First, it says that He will remove the vineyard's hedge and it will be consumed and that He will break down its wall and it will become trampled ground. This is the removal of the protective hedge. This may sound harsh, but Matthew 5 explains that it is the only possible consequence. It states that Christians are to be the salt of the earth and that if the salt loses it savor, it is good for nothing but to be trampled under the feet of men. One of the characteristics of salt is that it creates thirst. If we, as the salt of the earth, lose our ability to cause others to thirst after what we have, we will be good for nothing.

It seems that the Christians of our era have been far more concerned with comfort than with character. Our pursuit of comfort and disregard for integrity has done much damage to the Church, particularly where men are concerned. The TV ministry scandals of the late 1980s were not a unique phenomenon. They were caused by the same drive for comfort over character that plagues Christians today. Those TV ministries were unique only because they were in the national spotlight. Just as men mocked and scorned those fallen TV preachers, men are mocking and scorning lay believers because they, too, lack character. They have lost their savor. Because of our enormous lack of character, we are now being trodden under the feet of men. The Church is threatened more today than it ever has been because we have lost our ability to cause others to thirst for what we have.

If we allow our character deficiencies to run unabated, we will most certainly lose our protective hedge. If we let that happen, then we paint a bleak picture for ourselves. Consider that God initially builds a protective hedge in our lives to bring us closer to Him. If we fail to draw closer to God in spite of this protective hedge, we will fail to develop His character, a part of which is self-control, within ourselves. Verse five indicates that if we fail to produce the right kind of fruit in our lives, God will remove that protective hedge. The end result would be that we would lack self-control, just as we would lack the rest of God's character. In addition, we would be deprived of God's protective hedge. These two factors would add up to create a life-controlling habit. Sadly, it is quite common to find born-again people with uncontrollable habits. We could avoid such a bleak destiny if only we would allow the Spirit of God to prompt us to prayer.

Verse six continues to undo verse two. "And I will lay it waste; it will not be pruned or hoed, but briars and thorns will come up. I will also charge the clouds to rain no rain on it." Remember how in verse two God was working the soil, symbolic of conviction, and removing the stones, symbolic of salvation. After He finished that work, it began producing a crop of grapes. A degeneration followed, and it produced only weeds by the time we reach verses five and six. Then God even removed the possibility of any future growth by commanding that the clouds rain no rain on it. It creates the picture of someone completely barren where the things of God are concerned. He no longer produces anything of any value to God. With the removal of rain, the vineyard completely dries up and withers away into oblivion.

Verse seven concludes the parable, telling us that the vineyard is the house of Israel, the Jews. To the uninitiated or the uninformed in Isaiah's day, this would have been a shock. They were God's chosen people! Perhaps some believers today will be equally shocked to learn that the parable still represents God's people, but today it represents His Church.

My House Shall Be Called...

And Jesus entered the temple and cast out all those who were buying and selling in the temple, and overturned the tables of the moneychangers and the seats of those who were selling doves. And He said to them, "It is written, 'My house shall be called a house of prayer'; but you are making it a robbers' den" (Matt. 21:12,13).

When Jesus said, "My house shall be called a house of prayer," He made prayer preeminent. In other words, prayer should stand out over all other things in the house of God. The verse implies that if prayer is not preeminent, the house of God robs Him. Down through the ages, we have read this verse and felt that Jesus was angry because moneychangers were in the temple. The verse really deals with the prayerlessness of God's people and how prayerlessness allowed the house of God to become a place that robbed Him.

Without prayer we rob God, too. The pastor needs to know that if he does not pray, he robs God of what God could do through his ministry. The deacon that does not pray needs to know that he is robbing God through the decisions He could make through him. The Sunday school teacher needs to know that if there is no prayer in his life, God is robbed.

Jesus clarifies this in verse fourteen by healing the blind and the lame. Right after saying that the house of God had become a place that robbed God, He demonstrated by example what God would liked to have done in that place. He healed the blind and the lame. Clearly we are not trying to persuade a reluctant God to do things. God is trying to get a reluctant Church to pray. What Jesus did goes far beyond throwing out moneychangers; Jesus was throwing out thieves. In today's setting, we could say Jesus was throwing out people who do not pray.

The Fig Tree

Now in the morning, when He returned to the city, He became hungry. And seeing a lone fig tree by the road, He came to it, and found nothing on it except leaves only; and He said to it, "No longer shall there ever be any fruit from you." And at once the fig tree withered (Matt. 21:18,19).

The mention of Jesus being hungry in verse eighteen refers to His physical hunger, and yet in the context of this chapter we find that Jesus was also spiritually hungry. Just the day before, He had driven out the moneychangers from the "holy temple" which He denounced as a den of robbers. He had traveled to Jerusalem, the "holy city" and found only a spiritual wasteland. He wanted to do great things, but only a tiny minority shared His dreams and desires. To say the least, He was disappointed. When He spoke to the fig tree, He was speaking symbolically to God's people. Throughout the Old Testament, prophets had prophesied over God's people by using the fig tree as an illustration. The tree Jesus found that day bore nothing of value, just like God's people at the time. Today the scene is replayed in the spiritual realm over and over. When Jesus wants to draw from what our lives are producing, He often finds nothing of any value. From the lack of good fruit, we wither up just as the vineyard in Isaiah's parable.

When I was first saved, I went to my church expecting that anyone who had been saved for some time would be the perfect example for me to follow. I was quite surprised and dismayed at what I found. I found Christians that had gone to church for thirty years who, when put under pressure, could fly off the handle with the best of the heathen. This didn't make sense to me. I began to ask myself, "Where is the practical application of Christianity? There must be more to Christianity than just going to church." Even as a brand new Christian, I knew there had to be something more.

Developing the fruit of God's Spirit is a part of that "something more." That fruit was one of the things missing in the lives of those saints who had been saved for years. As a young Christian, I wondered, "How can they be like that after being saved for years?" This brings us back to prayer. Only through prayer do we develop the fruit of the Spirit. You can study the fruit of the Spirit in English, Greek, and Lower Slabovian. You can memorize them. You can have them mounted on the roof of your house on a flashing neon sign. But you will never develop them in your life without prayer. The fruit of the Spirit is the character of God. We never develop in the character of God without spending time in His presence. Proverbs says that if you spend time with an angry man you will become angry, and if you spend time with a wise man you will become wise. The spirit of the people we spend time with is contagious. No matter how impervious we think ourselves to be, it eventually begins to develop in us. Therefore, if we spend time in God's presence, His character begins to develop in us. When I realized this, things finally began to make sense. The reason there was little or no practical application of Christianity in those people's lives was because there was little or no prayer in their lives. It doesn't matter how long you've gone to church. The only thing that matters is how much time you spend in God's presence.

Fruit For Others

Do you know why a fruit tree bears fruit? It bears fruit for those creatures who do not have any and need some. It never bears fruit for itself. The tree does not need the fruit. The fruit is a natural result of a healthy union between the branch and the vine, but it is not for the tree. In like manner, God is not so concerned that we bear fruit for our sakes. It is for those around us that need to see Jesus.

Our children are purists. They see things through idealism. They do not need to hear dad raise his voice in worship during the church service and then hear him raise his voice in an angry fit at home a few minutes after church. Their response will be, "If that is all church did for dad, I don't need it. I'm not going to be a hypocrite." That's fruit for death. What our children need to see is dad being put under pressure and responding in a godly way before his flesh can react. They need to see dad respond to the Spirit of God which gently speaks to his heart and says, "A soft answer will turn away wrath." Our families need to see God's Spirit take control of our reactions. That's fruit for God.

It all goes back to how much time we are spending in the presence of God. We cannot focus in on a particular fruit and try to bring it about in our life. It would be useless for me to concentrate on producing peace in my life. Fruit trees don't sweat and strain to produce fruit. It happens naturally under the proper conditions ordained by God. All we need to do is place ourselves in conditions God ordained to make us fruitful. That means we must focus our attention on Jesus and spending time with Him. He will develop the fruit needed for our situations.

CHAPTER FOUR

Prayer And Intimacy

The knowledge of God is very far from the love of Him.
—Blaise Pascal

In all things, God seeks to show us the kind of relationship He desires to have with us. For example, marriage, the union of man and woman, has been given to us by God to teach us about the union of Christ and the Church. It is designed to show us how intimate God seeks to be with His church. The reason marriage won't be necessary in heaven is then we will fully understand our relationship with the Lord. In heaven, we will finally love everyone the way we love our mates.

> *For this cause a man shall leave his father and mother, and shall cleave to his wife; and the two shall become one flesh. This mystery is great; but I am speaking with reference to Christ and the church (Eph. 5:31,32).*

The reason the marriage relationship is often a great mystery to us is that we don't fully understand the relationship between Christ and His church. God has instituted this union to show us how beautiful our relationship with Him is to be.

The symbolic relationship between husband and wife and Christ and the Church may sound very simple at first, but it is not without its complexities. For example, in marriage, the husband represents Christ, and the wife represents the Church. That sounds simple enough. However, both husband and wife are a part of the bride of Christ. So the husband's role alternates between his role as Christ and his role as the Bride. The wife's position is more stable because her role as the Bride does not change.

In this chapter, we will look at the most important issue in our relationship with God and with our spouse: intimacy. In the marriage, intimacy is greatly expressed in sexual intercourse. In our relationship with God, intimacy is expressed in prayer. Intercourse in our relationship with our mate parallels prayer in our relationship with God. The sexual relationship is much more than simply a physical pleasure that God allows us to experience. It is a representation of the deep relationship God longs to have with us. To fully understand this, we need to engage in an elementary study of the Hebrew language.

The Yadah Relationship

The Hebrew word **yad** is a primary root word or a base word. **Yad** simply means "hand." Because it is a base word, you can change its meaning by adding a letter to it. If we add an "a" to the end of the word, the result is **yada**, which means "to know." An example of the word **yada** is found in Genesis 4:1: "Adam knew Eve his wife; and she conceived..." (KJV). The word "knew" in this verse is the word **yada**. Obviously, **yada** implies intimacy. If Adam knew (**yada**) Eve and she conceived, then we can easily see there was intimacy involved. Interestingly, **yad** ("hand"), the primary root of **yada**, plays a focal role in this intimacy. The hand is very involved in developing a relationship. First we hold hands, then we hug with our hands, and so forth. Even when we meet another person, we will shake hands. Since Adam knew Eve and she conceived, we can see right away that things had to go beyond just a hand shake. The intimacy of **yada** goes beyond the hand meeting the hand, to the flesh meeting the flesh.

If we add another letter to our word, we get still another meaning. If we attach an "h" to the end of **yada**, you get **yadah**. The word still deals with both the hand and intimacy, but it is different because it is used only in the context of God. The word **yadah** means to know God. It is used in Daniel 11:32: "...the people who know [**yadah**] their God will display strength and take action." Since this word also gets its meaning from the primary root word **yad**, the hand is also involved in its meaning. The word **yadah** implies the hand extended in prayer or praise. Through the extended hand we develop intimacy with God because throughout Scripture, it is the symbol of prayer. First Timothy 2:8 tells us to "pray, lifting up holy hands." The lifted hand, the sign of surrender, is the path to intimacy with God. So when the bride of Christ is giving herself to Christ in prayer, it is symbolic of the sexual act between husband and wife. Prayer is meant to be a very intimate thing. There must be as much intimacy in knowing God as there is in knowing your mate. So often we get to know all about God and yet never get to know God. Prayer is the only way to know the Father. This is best explained by the wedding ceremony.

Knowing God

The wedding ceremony is symbolic of someone giving his life to Christ. In the wedding ceremony, when the man and woman come to the altar and give their lives to each other, the Bible says they become one (Eph. 5:31,32). In this setting we have an earthly picture of a heavenly event. The wedding ceremony was instituted to help us understand what happens when a person gives his life to Christ. It is the picture of salvation. At the beginning of the ceremony, the man, who represents Christ, is at the altar. The woman, who represents the Church, is coming down the aisle to present herself to him. After the vows, they become one in the sight of God. A similar thing happens when someone gives his life to Christ. However, to go through the wedding ceremony means only that you are married. It does not automatically mean you know one another. Similarly, you can go through the ceremony of salvation, praying the sinner's prayer and accepting Christ into you heart (vowing your life to Christ), but that only means you are saved. It does not automatically mean that you know Christ intimately. Without intimacy, there isn't any knowing; there is only knowing about.

This is why Jesus made prayer preeminent. It's the same reason the sexual relationship is preeminent in the marriage. Without intimacy we can only know about one another. God is using the intimacy of our marriages to teach us the importance of prayer in our relationship with Him. Intimacy, in either relationship, produces that which God can use to keep us together.

> *Not everyone who says to Me, "Lord, Lord," will enter the kingdom of heaven; but he who does the will of My Father who is in heaven. Many will say to Me on that day, "Lord, Lord, did we not prophesy in Your name, and in Your name cast out demons, and in Your name perform many miracles?" And then I will declare to them, "I never knew you; DEPART FROM ME..."* (Matt. 7:21-23).

That is strong language! This has implications that without prayer and a deep relationship with God, you could be on shaky ground at best. Perhaps one of my own latter-day parables will clarify the situation. There was once a husband and wife that hadn't shared intimacy for months. One day at work, the husband got his great idea (husbands often get these great ideas) that tonight would be a perfect night to be with his wife intimately. When he got home, he walked into the kitchen and made his announcement, "Honey, I've decided that tonight's the night!" She looked at him and said, "Depart from me! I don't even know you. You worker of iniquity!" They were still married, but they had no relationship. That is the lesson of the last mentioned Scripture. You don't have to pray to be a Christian. Without prayer, you'll still be saved, but you will have no intimate relationship with God. Without intimacy with Christ, it could develop into a situation where your relationship is dissolved, as in the aforementioned Scripture.

In addition, if one lacks that relationship, he will be taking God's name in vain. When we think of using the Lord's name in vain, we tend to think of using His name as a curse word. The old rabbinical teachings had a vastly different interpretation of the sixth commandment, however. It is best explained in the following manner. The only woman in the world who can call herself Mrs. Ronald J. Auch is my wife. No other woman in the world can make that claim because they lack the necessary relationship to me. If another woman called herself Mrs. Ronald J. Auch, she would be using my name in vain. It would be useless. It would not get her any place (it barely gets my wife anywhere). This gives us a new light in which to interpret Jesus' words. Jesus is telling us that there are those who believe they will be able to enter heaven simply because they used the name of Jesus. They used His name to cast out demons and to do many miracles, but they lacked a proper, intimate relationship with Jesus. That's why He said, "I never knew you." Therefore, they were using His name in vain.

You might say that the person who doesn't pray, doesn't have a prayer. Intimacy is required in order to know someone. This is why Jesus gives prayer preeminence. The person who never prays has just as poor of a relationship with God as the couple who never share intimacy have with each other. Though prayer and intimacy are to have a priority in our relationships with God and our mates, they do not exist simply for the pleasure of the experience. Prayer can be an exciting experience, but the results of prayer can be even more exciting. The results of prayer in our relationship with God are what keep us praying.

CHAPTER FIVE

The Spirit Of Harlotry

Sin is essentially a departure from God.
—Martin Luther

Many men don't like to admit it, but it is true nonetheless. In any male-female relationship, the woman controls the level of intimacy. Men never control it. It is true that men tend to prod and pursue it, but the final decision is the woman's. This is analogous to Christ's relationship with His bride, the Church. Jesus, the husband, never determines the degree of intimacy He will have with the Church. Like any husband, He hints and prods at intimacy, but the final decision is always the prerogative of the Church.

Christ, the Pursuer

The wife does not have authority over her own body, but the husband does; and likewise also the husband does not have authority over his own body, but the wife does. Stop depriving [defrauding] one another, except by agreement for a time that you may devote yourselves to prayer... (1 Cor. 7:4,5).

According to this verse, if we deny our mate the right they have to us, we defraud the relationship. This is a rather well-known verse, particularly to men who are trying to persuade their wives to strive for a greater degree of intimacy. However, very few believers are stretching beyond that narrow scope with that verse. As we, the Bride, apply this verse to our relationship with Christ, the greatest dimensions of this verse are revealed. We are confronted with the sobering truth that the Church has been denying Jesus His right to us. **Jesus currently has a bride that refuses Him.** We simply do not desire intimacy with Him, subsequently He cannot get us to pray.

This sad fact is causing repercussions in our marriages today. The reason there are such great problems in our homes today is because there are great problems in the Church's relationship with Christ. The Christian home is simply a reflection of the Church's relationship with Christ. Since husband and wife represent Christ and the Church, it can do no more than mirror the Church's relationship with Christ. This does not go without exception. There are homes that function as they should, but they are relatively few, just as there are those who have an intimate relationship with Christ but they are the remnant. Women denying their husbands is just a reflection of the Church denying Christ's invitations to intimacy. It isn't natural for women to do this.

> *To the woman He said, "I will greatly multiply your pain in childbirth, in pain you shall bring forth children; yet your desire shall be for your husband (Gen. 3:16).*

God created the woman with a natural desire for her husband. There is supposed to be a natural longing for your mate. However, through refusing your mate, you defraud the relationship. Defrauding the relationship removes the natural desire that is supposed to be there. I am not trying to point out a problem with today's Christian wife. This is a spiritual issue. It's not the woman's fault that the desire is gone—it's the Church's fault. The Church has defrauded her relationship with Christ, hence there is no desire for prayer.

Understanding God's Heart

When the Lord first spoke through Hosea, the Lord said to Hosea, "Go, take to yourself a wife of harlotry, and have children of harlotry; for the land commits flagrant harlotry, forsaking the Lord" (Hos. 1:2).

In the Book of Hosea, we find God instructing the prophet to marry Gomer, a prostitute. Hosea became a living object lesson to the people of Israel. He married a wife that he knew was going to leave him. Through his own grief, the people of the land were to gain an understanding of God's grief. The grief we experience through the lack of intimacy with our mates is to teach **us** of the grief God endures when **we** don't pray. Our lack of prayer is seen by God as His bride playing the harlot. Today's prayerless Church is "Gomer."

So My people are bent on turning from Me. Though they [prophets] call them to the One on high, none at all exalts Him. How can I give you up, O Ephraim? How can I surrender you, O Israel? How can I make you like Admah? How can I treat you like Zeboiim? My heart is turned over within Me, all my compassions are kindled (Hos. 11:7,8).

God was showing His people how hurt He was by their rejection (prayerlessness) of Him. He explained His anguish when He said, "How can I give you up, O Ephraim...Israel? How can I make you like Admah...treat you like Zeboiim?" Admah and Zeboiim were two cities that were geographically close to Sodom and Gomorrah which were destroyed when judgment came to Sodom and Gomorrah. God didn't want the same fate to befall His people, but He knew that their destiny was judgment if they would not turn back to Him.

God was grief-stricken, and He is today, too, because the same thing is happening with His people. They are rejecting Him. They want no intimacy with Him. They do not pray.

By translating the situation into the marriage, we can also understand God's heart in this matter. Men can relate to God's heart when they approach their wives intimately and are denied. Their feelings of frustration and rejection are to demonstrate to them the pain God feels when they refuse to pray. A women can relate to God's heart when she discovers that her husband has been unfaithful or involved in pornography, alcohol, or anything that takes their affections from their wives. The wife's feelings of rejection and frustration are the same as God's feelings when they refuse to pray.

Spirit of Harlotry vs. Spirit of Prayer

Their deeds will not allow them to return to their God.
For a spirit of harlotry is within them, and they do not
know the Lord (Hos. 5:4).

Their own spirit of harlotry prevented them from experiencing intimacy with God, for it says, "...they do not know the Lord." Today the situation is largely the same. There is a great spiritual battle taking place between that same spirit of harlotry, or lust, and the spirit of prayer or intimacy. The spirit of harlotry is drawing us away from God. It is a self-seeking attitude, while the spirit of prayer is a selfless one. When we are enticed by our own lusts and yield to this spirit of harlotry, we lose interest in others. Instead, we are preoccupied with our own desires and all the things we want for ourselves. This is nothing less than the defrauding of relationships.

In such a context, it is easy to see how, as husband and wife, defrauding our relationship with our mate parallels being a Christian (Christ's bride) and a friend of the world. The world is the other god we are pursuing. The world teaches us to seek the immediate gratification of all our desires.

What is the source of quarrels and conflicts among you?
Is not the source your pleasures [lusts] that wage war in
your members? You lust and do not have; so you commit

murder. And you are envious and cannot obtain; so you fight and quarrel. You do not have because you do not ask. You ask and do not receive, because you ask with wrong motives, so that you may spend it on your pleasures. You adulteresses, [harlots], do you not know that friendship with the world is hostility toward God? Therefore whoever wishes to be a friend of the world makes himself an enemy of God (James 4:1-4).

Note that in verse 2 it says, "You lust and do not have; so you commit murder." Most are inclined to say, "I've never committed murder." Don't be so sure. The spirit of harlotry or lust is self-seeking. Love is self-less. When two people become one there is to be an equal giving of each for the other because love is selfless. However, when one member of that party has a lustful spirit, they become very self-centered. That selfishness kills the kindred spirit for their mate. Instead of a mutual intimate meeting, intimately the kindred spirit of the mate is repelled. "You lust and do not have; so you commit murder."

The last part of verse 2 says, "You do not have because you do not ask." James teaches one of the most important aspects on prayer we can learn here. He says the reason you don't have the thing you desire is because you do not ask for it. This clearly is a reference to something in the will of God. If it is as simple as asking for it and receiving it, it is something God wills for you to have. Keeping with the context of these verses, he's dealing with the intimacy between husband and wife. It is clearly God's will for husband and wife to share intimacy.

Verse 3 throws us for a loop. Right after saying in verse 2 that all you need to do to receive it is to ask for it, verse 3 says when you ask, you don't receive. Then it tells us why: "...because you ask with wrong motives, so that you may spend it on your pleasures." James is telling us that you can be in the center of God's will and not receive the very thing you pray for because of wrong motives. God is just as interested in the pray-er as He is in what you are praying for. Here

He tells us that He will not answer a prayer that is in His will if there is something in the pray-er's life that is not right (i.e., wrong motives [lust]).

Materialism vs. Sensuality

For all that is in the world, the lust of the flesh and the lust of the eyes and the boastful pride of life, is not from the Father, but is from the world (1 John 2:16).

When we consider the bride of Christ, we find it is made up of both men and women. Each have their particular area of lust. Women seem to be drawn to the things that cover her flesh. Men seem to be drawn to that which satisfies his flesh. For the woman it is materialism (lust of the eyes), for the men it is sensuality (lust of the flesh). I believe men have been given a bad deal. They certainly have their problems with lust, but I do not believe it is any greater than the problems women have with lust. A glance back at Hosea's wife, Gomer, demonstrates this.

For their mother [Gomer] has played the harlot; she who conceived them has acted shamefully. For she said, "I will go after my lovers, who give me my bread and my water, my wool and my flax, my oil and my drink (Hos. 2:5).

Gomer pursued her lovers not from a great sexual lust but rather from a material lust. She wanted her wool and flax, her oil and drink.

Consider how the bride of Christ has responded to the popular faith message, with its primary focus on getting things from God. We, like Gomer, have been enticed by our own material lusts. It is very typical for the bride to be attracted to that which makes her attractive. However, when the message of Christ the pursuer is presented, we are disinterested. That message is built upon selflessness. That's something we want to avoid because we are self-centered.

The two greatest causes of arguments in the marriage

today are money and sex. The woman marries with warm thoughts (lusts) of material comfort. Her dreams are of a house and clothes. The man marries with warm thoughts (lusts) of sex. His dreams are of intimacy every night. The wife enters the marriage thinking that her husband wants to live and breath to provide her with every material thing she wants. The man enters the marriage assuming his wife will want to make use of the bedroom every night just as he does. Then, just as the Scripture states, the source of quarrels and conflict among us is from the lusts that wage war in our members.

If a woman wants to understand how a man feels about sex (lust of the flesh) she must compare it to her desire to go shopping (lust of the eyes). Ladies, does the phrase "shop until you drop" mean anything to you? I never could figure out how a woman could get any pleasure out of window shopping until I compared the lust of the eyes to my desire to fulfill the flesh. Most women cannot understand what kind of pleasure a man can get out of looking at a pornographic magazine until they compare the lust of the flesh to their own lust of the eyes.

The practice of either the lust of the flesh or the lust of the eyes engulfs us in the pride of life. Suddenly, this life means more to us than our relationship with Christ. Suddenly, a man will throw away his relationship with his wife and Christ to have an affair.

The Church today is very much wrapped up with the pride of life. This is evident by its unwillingness to give up this life to seek the life of Christ. We will not pray. We cannot give ourselves to Christ because that would mean death to the life we now live. Hosea 5:4 said our deeds will not allow us to return to God. Verse 5 tells us why: "the pride of Israel testifies against him." The pride of life keeps us from prayer. It keeps us enmeshed in our own lusts.

The only thing that will bring our homes into the relationship God desires us to have, is for the Church to go back to prayer. Our return to prayer will restore the spirit of intimacy and break the spirit of harlotry that controls our nation. However, the only thing that will bring the Church back to prayer is a spirit of repentance. The problem with repentance is that it is difficult. Repentance hurts. Genesis 3:16 says, "...In pain you shall bring forth children...." Our repentance must crush our spirit to the same extent that our sin has crushed God's Spirit.

CHAPTER SIX

The Bitter Heart

*Nothing sets a person so much out of the devil's reach as
humility.*
—Jonathan Edwards

It stings a little to admit it, but most of the problems we
Christians face in our homes, particularly the lack of intimacy, are a consequence of our own pride, the very sin which
ruined many of God's own angels. At its base, pride is self-
centeredness, a preoccupation with self. Pride ignores others'
hurts and needs and focuses exclusively on the needs, wants,
and whims of self. Even worse, as was demonstrated by
Satan's rebellion, pride concentrates on self even to the exclusion of God, to one extent or another. When a man is bound
tightly in the clutches of his own pride, he will become very
bitter if he perceives himself to be wronged. Our pride allows
a spirit of harlotry to run rampant in our marriages, destroying the intimacy of our wedlock. Ironically, as we intensely
strive to fulfill ourselves, that very drive deprives us of what
we seek. As Jesus said, "He who seeks to gain his life will lose
it."

Evangelist John Collins of Dallas, Texas once brought

out a beautiful truth concerning this issue of bitterness. Believers needn't respond with bitterness when they are wronged. Bitterness and a desire for vengeance are expressions of a man's pride which breeds his insistence to control his own affairs. God doesn't want His people to have anything to do with such behavior. Rather He wants His people to grow in humility which is selflessness, the opposite of pride which is selfishness. When the humble man is wronged, he will seek his God and let God handle his problems.

Suffering For Doing Right: Jesus

Without humility, there is no way we can respond as God wants us to when we suffer for doing right. As a child, I was taught that if you do something wrong, you will pay a price for it. I never really enjoyed suffering because of my mischief, but I never had a problem with it either because I knew my actions warranted punishment. When I was old enough to drive, if I were stopped by the police and fined because I was speeding, I simply accepted that as paying the price for wrong doing. I knew I was getting what I deserved. My problem came when I had to suffer for doing right. I knew I didn't deserve suffering for a good deed. Paying a price for doing right is much more difficult to deal with.

Jesus is the greatest example of someone paying a price for right doing.

> *Therefore, since we have so great a cloud of witnesses surrounding us, let us also lay aside every encumbrance, and the sin which so easily entangles us, and let us run with endurance the race that is set before us, fixing our eyes on Jesus, the author and perfecter of faith, who for the joy set before Him endured the cross, despising the shame, and has sat down at the right hand of the throne of God (Heb. 12:1,2).*

When Jesus was brought before Pilate, He had done no wrong. Jesus did no evil, only good. Yet His beard was ripped from His face. A crown of thorns was jammed on His head.

He was dressed in a scarlet robe and ridiculed. He received forty lashes with a Roman cat-of-nine-tails. In His battered condition, He was forced to carry His own cross. He died in an agonizing crucifixion. He suffered incredibly for doing right.

Jesus set an example for us to show us how we should behave when we are persecuted for doing good. He humbled himself and sought God. He didn't even try to defend himself against the flimsy and ludicrous charges of His accusers. He set His eyes on the joy set before Him. Jesus had His eyes fixed on eternity, on His Father, not on the suffering of the moment. More often than not, we are so unlike Him. We have our eyes fixed on the present, and, even more incriminating, we have our eyes fixed on ourselves.

Even as He was suffering unbearable anguish on the cross, Jesus was challenged. "You who are going to destroy the temple and rebuild it in three days, save yourself. If you are the Son of God, come down from the cross," they cried. Nonetheless, Jesus endured because of the joy set before Him. Today He is at the right hand of the Father.

> ...My son, do not regard lightly the discipline of the Lord, nor faint when you are reproved by Him; for those whom the Lord loves He disciplines... (Heb. 12:5,6).

Generally when we think of discipline, we think of it in terms of punishment for wrong doing. However to keep contextually true, we find this portion of Scripture challenging us to keep our eyes on Jesus. Christ did not suffer discipline because of wrong doing but rather because of right doing. The discipline of the Lord in this setting is that of suffering for the sake of character development.

> For they [earthly fathers] disciplined us for a short time as seemed best to them, but He disciplines us for our good, that we may share His holiness [character development] (Heb. 12:10).

It is not punishment for wrong doing, it is deferring your

gratification. Richard Foster in his book, *Celebration of Discipline*, defines discipline as, "deferred gratification." If you will discipline yourself (deny yourself) now, you will reap the benefits of it later.

> *All discipline for the moment seems not to be joyful, but sorrowful; yet to those who have been trained by it, afterwards it yields the peaceful fruit of righteousness (Heb. 12:11).*

Pride will not allow us to get along with other people, but humility will. The discipline God allows us to go through is to teach us how to treat other people the way God treats us. We are to bear the peaceful fruit of righteousness. Righteousness has to do with our relationships with other men. Godliness has to do with our relationship with God. Therefore the righteous man treats other men the way God would. Any ungodly man can repay evil for evil. Any ungodly man can repay good for good. Only the righteous man can repay good for evil. Only the righteous man will put up with suffering for being right.

Suffering for Doing Right: God's People

> *Pursue peace with all men, and the sanctification without which no one will see the Lord (Heb. 12:14).*

We are admonished to pursue peace with all men, which would be the bearing of the "peaceful fruit of righteousness." We are also asked to pursue sanctification. Sanctification is being set apart. In this case, it would refer to living in a different realm than the ungodly. How we treat the ungodly separates us from their world. The moment you return good for evil you are instantly separated from the world of the ungodly. If you will suffer for being right and do not allow your own pride to cause bitterness to develop in your heart, you will find that the fruit of your righteousness will be sanctification. In essence, if you suffer for being right and don't try to get even, one day you will reap tremendous benefits. That is what Jesus did and now He sits at the right hand of the Father.

If a person is right, but then wronged, he can become very bitter. Let's consider another man who suffered for being right, Joseph. Joseph is given a coat of many colors by his parents. This begins to rub his brothers the wrong way. Then Joseph has two dreams that indicate his whole family will one day bow down to him. This irritates his brothers even more. One day Joseph's brothers sell him into slavery.

Joseph is eventually purchased by Potiphar. One day while Potiphar is away, his wife tries to seduce Joseph. She hands herself to him on a silver platter. If Joseph had been a bitter man he would have rationalized his thinking here. He could have said, "I wronged no one. I didn't ask them to give me a special coat. I didn't ask God to give me those dreams. I have done no wrong. I'm tired of being wronged while I am actually right."

This is where most men are stopped in their tracks today. Because of the serious problems with intimacy in the marriage, many men feel wronged though they are right. It is right for them to have their mate intimately. However, through the refusal of their mate, they feel wronged. At this point they start thinking, "I'm tired of being denied by my own wife all the time." Then the philosophy of the world sets in. "Go ahead," it says. "Do it for yourself. You're worth it. You are somebody. You deserve it after all that you have been through." With that type of thinking the bitter man will make a rash decision that could change his whole life.

Joseph was not a bitter man. Joseph was a humble man who sought his God. Joseph did not esteem himself above his God. Joseph responds to Potiphar's wife, "How then could I do this great evil, and sin against God?" (Gen. 39:9). The man who will go to his God when he is wronged finds that God becomes the fulfillment of his life. That is why when Joseph was tempted, his first thought was of his God. His own desires came second to his God.

The man who will not seek his God when he is wronged finds that his own self-serving desires become the only fulfillment of his life. The basic reason for not having a well developed prayer life is from self-centeredness. When a self-centered person is denied his rights, he becomes bitter. A bitter person can sell his soul in a moment's time. Joseph had an uncle, Esau, whose life was nearly ruined because of bitterness.

> *See to it that no one comes short of the grace of God; that no root of bitterness springing up causes trouble, and by it many be defiled; that there be no immoral or godless person like Esau, who sold his own birthright for a single meal (Heb. 12:15,16).*

Joseph's bitter uncle sold his birthright for a single meal. The bitter person will make a rash decision based on vengeance.

See to it that no one comes short of the grace of God. When the apostle Paul prayed that the thorn would be removed from his life, God said, "My grace is sufficient for thee" (2 Cor. 12:9). God wants us to live by His grace. Prayer activates God's grace. Without prayer we struggle in the application of the grace of God. In prayer you find that God becomes the sustaining power we must have.

There are many things in this life that are not fair at all. But that doesn't matter because the grace of God is sufficient to carry us through this life. If we will just fix our eyes on Jesus, who, for the joy set before Him, endured the cross, we will find hope in a hopeless world. When you are wronged, humble yourself and pray for God will give grace to the humble but He will resist the proud.

CHAPTER SEVEN

No Repentance

We must remember who and what we are as a people, lest we lose our sense of identity, and, as a result, lose ourselves.
—*Otto von Bismarck*

Calvin Olson had been a missionary to Bangladesh for many years. He had returned to the United States to itinerate and raise funds several times before. This time, however, was different because this time he had to spend an evening in London before continuing on to America. It's not that he had anything to complain about. Quite the contrary. The motel room he stayed in, though a bit modest and austere by British standards, seemed luxurious to a man accustomed to the rigors of life in Bangladesh. His eyes came to rest on the far side of the room, on the television in the corner. It had been a long time since he'd viewed any Western TV. He sensed a voice beckoning—no, tempting—him to turn on the set and see what he had been missing while he was on the mission field. He strolled over and turned on the television, which erupted in the strained convulsive laughter of a simulated studio audience. As he was watching the television show, the Holy Spirit spoke clearly and quietly to him, "Have you forgotten who you are?" With that, he turned the set off.

It is a question which the Church of Jesus Christ in the West should ask itself. Have we forgotten who we are? Who are we anyway? To begin with, we are Christians. That means we have Christ (literally translated "the anointed one") in us. Being a Christian also means that we do not own ourselves. We are His. Christ is the one who paid the ultimate price for us, His virgin bride.

That last item is probably the most revealing about our identity. We were washed with His blood and stand before Him as His bride. We are referred to as His virgin bride because the marriage supper of the Lamb has not yet taken place. When we think of the word "virgin," images of purity, newness, and naivete come to mind. However, there is another quality of a virgin which explains who we are. It is that of being set apart. The virgin's greatest desire is to keep herself for her prospective groom and no one else. In the same way, as the virgin bride of Christ, our lives are to be devoted to Jesus.

> *...And the woman who is unmarried, and the virgin, is concerned about the things of the Lord, that she may be holy both in body and spirit... (1 Cor. 7:34).*

Paul told the church in Corinth that it should be their aim to be devoted to the Lord in both body and spirit. Today I think we're falling short in that respect. To be sure, we do concentrate on being devoted to the Lord in spirit. We worship in spirit, we pray in spirit, we sing in the spirit. We expend great energy trying to tune in to the spiritual realm. That is important. Paul said it was. But there is a physical part of our devotion to God that is just as important, and Paul said that, too. Today we are missing it: devotion in body. When that aspect of our devotion is overlooked, as it is today, we forget who we are: we are those who are to be devoted to Christ. Therefore, our involvement in worldliness is seen by our Lord as betraying Him. In fact, it's even worse than that. He perceives us playing the role of the harlot if we are intimately involved in the world as believers.

> *For I am jealous for you with a godly jealousy; for I betrothed you to one husband, that to Christ I might present you as a pure virgin. But I am afraid, lest the serpent deceived Eve by his craftiness, your minds should be led astray from the simplicity and purity of devotion to Christ (2 Cor. 11:2,3).*

The Greek word translated "devotion" here implies giving of one's self without reserve. There is no holding of anything for yourself. It's a complete abandoning of self in a most sincere, simple, upright fashion. It is simple and needs very little explanation. Things become complicated only when we get involved with the world, for then we do not wish to admit that our devotion is waning. We maintain with great vigor that, in spite of our ever increasing involvement with the world, we are one hundred percent devoted to God. It is a very complex theology that we need to formulate in order to justify our involvement in the world. That takes a lot of explaining, and a lot of twisting of the Scripture. What results is a wishy-washy, convoluted theology, difficult (if not impossible) for an outsider to understand. True devotion needs no complex explanation, however.

What is happening to us is nothing new. Man's devotion to God has been drained by his love for the world since the very beginning. Take Eve, for example. She was devoted to God, and, so far as we know, never sinned. But she was distracted by the lust of the eyes. The world and all it held drew her eyes away from her pure devotion to God. Today, the world and all it holds has drawn the Bride's eyes off of Christ. We have strayed so far from the thought of devotion to Christ that we spend more time justifying our lifestyles than concerning ourselves with the intimacy of our relationship with Christ.

But Eve wasn't in it alone, and neither are we. From Eve's first sin to our most recent one, mankind has been deceived by Satan's cunning and subtlety. He didn't say to

Eve, "Come, eat of this fruit. Then your pain in child birth will be greatly multiplied, and you shall be cast out of this lovely garden. Yes, where you go, the ground will be cursed because of you, and it shall bear both thorns and thistles for you. What you eat will be the consequence of great toil and hardship. You will be separated from God, which will deeply hurt Him, and that is the goal of my existence." Satan doesn't come in and announce his intentions. We never sense him saying, "Greetings, I am Lucifer and these are the hordes of hell, all of us destined to writhe for eternity in a lake of sulfur. Come join us." He would never successfully tempt anyone that way. Instead, he attracts us very subtly, through our own lusts. Satan attracts us through a harlot spirit.

The Harlot Spirit in Marriage

When a man or a woman attracts another person's spouse away from their mate, they do so through a harlot spirit. It is a very serious business which does not leave room for or warrant tactful euphemisms, so I'm going to be quite blunt. First of all, we must call things as they are. If a woman is having sex with another woman's husband, she is what God calls a harlot. That is very basic and simple. It becomes complicated only when such a woman tries to justify her involvement in such an affair by saying things like, "I just got caught up in the moment," or "It's not my fault; my husband is not meeting my needs because he's always away on business. I was thrust into it." Still, the pure simple truth is it is a spirit of harlotry.

If an individual has a problem, what the Bible calls an evil desire or a lust, he can easily be attracted when he encounters this harlot spirit. He can easily be drawn away by his own lusts. Although I will refer to the harlot as a she, this harlot can operate through a man just as well as it can through a woman. Men are attracting women away at the same rate women are attracting men away.

But each one is tempted when he is carried away and enticed by his own lust. Then when lust has conceived, it gives birth to sin; and when sin is accomplished, it brings forth death (James 1:14,15).

Our God is a legal God. By that, I do not mean we should be legalists, following the Old Testament law like the Pharisees and the teachers of the law did in Jesus' day. We are in the day of grace. All I mean is that our God will do nothing illegally. He will not tamper with or violate the moral and spiritual laws He has established. He sacrificed His only Son in an agonizing crucifixion instead of violating His laws concerning the legal cleansing of sins. Jesus had to die and shed His blood in order for our sins to be legally cleansed away.

According to God's law, a mate can demand exclusive devotion, especially in the area of intimacy. Very few mates are willing to share their spouses with another person sexually. The harlot spirit, on the other hand, is willing to share intimacy with another woman's property. So she is willing, for the time being, to allow the man to maintain intimacy with his wife and with her also. The harlot doesn't ask for exclusive rights over the man because he is not her husband. But that is only a temporary condition. She traps or entices the man through the willingness of her own flesh. Her willingness drags the man away through his own lusts. However, she realizes that she cannot make great demands of exclusiveness yet because legally she does not own him.

The wife has every right to demand exclusiveness. She is not willing to share her husband with any other woman. Therefore, referring back to James, when the affair is found out (when the lust has conceived) the wife feels so violated that she is repulsed at the thought of intimacy with her husband (the lust gives birth to sin). The intimacy of the marriage is killed through the revelation of sin. The reason for the destruction of the intimacy is to test the repentance of the man.

At this point, the harlot can make her most deadly move. Knowing the wife has cut off intimacy, she will continue to entice. The husband who has been cut off from his wife can either turn his thoughts on the harlot who waits for him with open arms, or he can genuinely repent and stay with his wife.

Then James says, "And when sin is accomplished it brings forth [gives birth] death." Once the wife has found out about the affair, or once the desire has given birth to sin, the man has an opportunity to repent and return to her. If he does, it will be relatively easy to restore that marriage; that is, easier than if he doesn't repent. If he continues his relationship with the harlot (when the sin has been accomplished), then that sin will give birth to death, which is separation from God. It is very common for a man who willingly sins over a long period of time to feel distanced from God. This will make it very difficult for him to repent. That's because it's easiest to repent when one senses intimacy with Christ; that is, Him drawing you to himself and away from your sin. But when God seems so far away and a man doesn't sense Him drawing him from sin, he has a very difficult time turning from his evil. He can still repent, but it won't be easy. He'll just have to take God at His word, because there will be very little emotion to motivate him.

If the husband does repent, his repentance will be put to the test by his wife's sexual abstinence. She can no longer give herself to her husband intimately because she feels so violated by his adultery. The desire conceived has given birth to sin, killing the relationship. The husband will find that the very thing he pursued in the harlot is denied to him by his mate. If he can stay with his mate, even though he is being denied, then his repentance is genuine. He will pursue God no matter what. He is rejecting his evil desires in order to follow the Lord.

If, on the other hand, the husband refuses to leave the harlot, there will be no other way out for him. The distance he senses between himself and God will remain there. He will find repentance only when he forsakes the harlot and goes back to his wife unconditionally.

The Harlot Spirit in the Church

Everything I have said about the harlot in marriage was to bring us to this point. Nothing I said about the harlot was designed to hurt anybody, but rather to give us an example from which to proceed. God is in the business of restoring, so how can my desire be less than to do the same?

We're going to turn the tables and look at this from another perspective, from Christ's perspective. We are His virgin bride, awaiting our marriage. We are to be devoted entirely to Him. Then Satan enters the picture, playing the role of the harlot, trying to entice us from our husband, Jesus. Satan is very cunning. He doesn't appear in reptilian form breathing sulfur. He disguises himself as the world, a much more subtle and innocent approach. If we do not have complete devotion to Christ, we will be enticed to him by our own lust for the world.

Like the harlot in marriage, Satan will allow us to be intimate with Christ and him at the same time—but only for a while. Satan knows that legally we are Christ's, so he will be content to temporarily share us with Him. The enemy knows that when we surrendered our lives to Christ, we gave Christ the legal right to us. However, Satan also knows that if we will continue to violate our relationship with God by allowing our lust to entice us, he will one day have legal rights to us.

James said, "When lust has conceived, it gives birth to sin." God, in His mercy, seems to allow us many opportunities for repentance. He will allow us to pursue other lovers for a period of time. If we do not heed the Holy Spirit's prompting, forsake this world and return to our God, He will eventually give us over to our lovers. Whenever God gave anyone over to their lovers in the Bible, they were eventually consumed by them. Ironically, the very thing they pursued became the worst thing that ever happened to them. That is why it is an act of mercy for God to allow us many opportunities for repentance. God will allow us intimacy with Him for a time, even though we are involved with sin. That intimacy gives us many chances to hear Him calling us away from our sin. Suppose God were to turn us over to our other lover the first time we sinned. We'd all be in a mess. But God in His mercy says, "I don't like what's going on, but I'm going to give you another chance to repent." But He only does this for a while. Eventually, He stops giving us chances to repent, just as He did the idolatrous nation of Israel.

> Thus I shall judge you, like women who commit adultery or shed blood are judged; and I shall bring on you the blood of wrath and jealousy. I shall also give you into the hands of your lovers, and they will tear down your shrines, demolish your high places, strip you of your clothing, take away your jewels, and will leave you naked and bare (Ezek. 16:38,38).

If we do not repent, God will finally give us over to the thing we so diligently sought. Inevitably the thing we sought is death. It is spiritual, emotional, and psychological death, and sometimes physical death also. If we don't repent, we are ultimately hoisted on our petard.

The New Testament is as explicit about these things as the Old Testament. Jesus said, "When sin is accomplished, it brings forth death." In writing to the believers at Corinth, Paul said that if a man persists in sin, we are to

> ...deliver such a one to Satan for the destruction of his flesh, that his spirit may be saved in the day of the Lord Jesus (1 Cor. 5:5).

This doesn't mean God is giving up on any one. He's only saying, "If you won't allow Me to destroy your sinful nature, then your own indulgence in sin will destroy it." After we gorge ourselves in our sin, we come to our senses. It breaks us and brings us to the altar with the knowledge that we need our God. Once a man is handed over to Satan, his flesh (sinful nature) is destroyed. He becomes consumed by his own sin. It is at this point that Satan will no longer allow intimacy with God. This is why a man can no longer sense God calling him to repentance. If he continues to resist God's proddings to repent, rejecting them year after year, he will be handed over to Satan who will refuse to allow him to hear God's voice. He will say, "It's just me and you now. No more hearing from God." Man loses his ability to repent, at least for a while.

> *For in the case of those who have once been enlightened and have tasted of the heavenly gift and have been made partakers of the Holy Spirit, and have tasted the good word of God and the powers of the age to come, and then have fallen away, it is impossible to renew them again to repentance, since they again crucify to themselves the Son of God, and put Him to open shame (Heb. 6:4-6).*

There remains no more repentance, meaning they cannot just say, "Jesus, I'm bound in sin. So let's forget this thing ever happened and start over. I want to be saved all over again from the beginning." But the passage from Hebrews tells us this is impossible. You cannot be renewed to the same sense of repentance as when you were first saved. If there is great sin, if full-grown sin has given birth to death, it must be dealt with. You cannot crucify Christ again by trying to avoid dealing with your sin through becoming born again, again.

Let me give you an example. I know of an individual who cheated on his wife. Because of that, his wife wouldn't allow him to live in the same house with her. One day, the man called his wife and said, "How long are you going to punish me? When will you allow me to return home? Why don't you just forget that this affair ever happened and let me come back home?" His wife, like any wife would, wanted nothing more than to let him return. She didn't want their relationship terminated. She wanted it to be healed. But she was waiting for him to repent. Up to this point, the man had figured that his wife would only be angry for a little while, then she would forget it. He hadn't gone to anyone for forgiveness. He hadn't gone to his wife for forgiveness, nor had he sought it from his church. He wasn't able to sense repentance because he hadn't dealt with these issues. Those issues had to be addressed, but as God says, "It is impossible to renew them again to repentance."

Forgiveness and Repentance: the Difference

There is something important for us to grasp here. It is impossible to renew them again to repentance—but not to forgiveness. They can still be forgiven. Often I have heard people say this verse means that you can reach a point at which God will no longer forgive you. However, nowhere in the verse is forgiveness mentioned. It is dealing with repentance. Repentance is something we do. Forgiveness is something God does. We mustn't confuse the two. God cannot repent for us, and we cannot forgive our own sin.

Devoted to God, or to the Good Life?

When you turn on the TV, do you ever ask yourself, "Does this enhance my relationship with Christ? Can this be considered devotion to Christ, sitting around listening to people swearing, cursing and mocking my God?" Often we become preoccupied with living the good life, enjoying ourselves and being entertained. We don't even consider how our pleasures effect our relationship with God. That's the last thing on our minds.

A Bible college student told me a story that confirmed this. He and some of his friends were driving around looking for something to do. There wasn't much going on at the college since most of the student body had gone to a Christian roller-skating rink. They really didn't want to go skating, so they were left with nothing to do. Finally, as they were driving through the city's hot-spot, they saw another group of students street-witnessing. Suddenly, it hit them. There was plenty to do. They parked their car and spent the rest of the evening telling people about Christ.

Our devotion is so far removed from Christ these days that serving Him is the farthest thing from our minds. Serving God is something we do when there is nothing else to do. We are devoted to the good life. We are committed to entertainment. I have heard of church elders that will spend money to rent some of Hollywood's "best" movies to watch on their VCRs as a family activity. I'm not talking about Christian-based movies, but rather regular Hollywood movies starring actors who hate God and anything Christian. Then we wonder why there is so much rebellion in today's church kids.

I'm not talking about whether these activities are "sinful" or not, but rather about whether or not they enhance my devotion to Christ.

Presumptuous Sins

Also keep back Thy servant from presumptuous sins; let them not rule over me... (Ps. 19:13).

We live in a day of presumptuous sins. We presume upon the grace of God. We sin cavalierly, know God will forgive us of any offense. King David prayed that he would be kept from such willful sin. It is the sin which is intentional or voluntary, committed over and over because the sinner presumes on God's grace. It's the kind of sin which spawned the old saying, "It is easier to get forgiveness than permission."

I remember counseling with a young couple in Ogden, Utah. The wife was sharing with me how her husband constantly did things that irritated her. She said, "I have told him over and over that doing those things drives me crazy, but he won't listen to me. He still does the same things."

I turned to the man and asked him if it was true. He said, "Yes, it's true."

I said, "If you know that doing certain things makes her upset, then why do you keep doing them?"

He said, "Because I know she'll keep forgiving me." He presumed upon his wife's forgiving nature and that poisoned their relationship for a long time.

"How petty!" I thought, a little arrogantly. Then I hear the Lord say, "Yes, but how many times have you done the same thing to Me? And how much has that hurt our relationship?"

We must get away from this selfish attitude, especially

in our relationship with God. We must stop selfishly taking advantage of God's grace as we do in order to indulge our flesh. We must determine that we won't act out of self-interest, no longer basing our actions on what feels pleasurable. Instead we must be guided by our devotion to Christ, doing the things that glorify Him.

> For you were called to freedom, brethren; only do not turn your freedom into an opportunity for the flesh, but through love serve one another (Gal. 5:13).

We must develop this kind of attitude, the attitude of the servant. We must pray as David did. His prayer was, "Keep me from willful sins." David understood the mercy of God, but chose not to take advantage of it. Rather he devoted himself to His God. Today we tend to take advantage of grace, doing things that we know we shouldn't, knowing that God will forgive us of it.

I think we have forgotten who we are. We are the virgin Bride. We are to live in complete devotion to Jesus. When we have intimate involvement with a world that opposes Jesus, we are being enticed by our own lusts; that's the way Jesus sees it. It's not complicated. It's just a simple fact.

The Overcomer

For many years I tried to become victorious over my sin by standing firm against it. I tried to exercise my own strength over it. It got me no where. The only victories I have ever experienced have come through devotion to Christ. Our battle against sin is only as effective as our devotion to Christ.

I don't need to become the best pray-er in the church. I don't need to become the most effective witness in the church. I don't need to be the top theologian in the church. I need one thing. I need to set my eyes on Jesus and be taken up entirely with Him. There is no other way to be an overcomer but to be taken up entirely with Jesus.

CHAPTER EIGHT

Knowing God: Knowing Your Spouse

Whenever intimacy is developed in a relationship, there are certain results you can look for. Whether it is intimacy with God or with your mate, the results are the same in both relationships.

Communication: It's Not Enough By Itself

Communication is probably one of the most important keys to knowing someone. Obviously communication is imperative to a good marriage. When you communicate you are learning about each other. You learn of each other's characteristics and qualities and that does a lot for the relationship. However, communication cannot be all that's needed to make up a fulfilling union.

Along with having good times of communication, there must be intimacy. In fact without intimacy, communication will always be hindered. Just as intimacy parallels prayer, communication parallels reading God's Word. When we read from God's Word, we are learning about God. We learn of His characteristics and qualities. However, I cannot get to know God through His word any more than I can know my wife by having only nice conversations around the dining room table. There must be intimacy before any knowing can take place.

> *But his delight is in the law of the Lord, and in His law*
> *he meditates day and night (Ps. 1:2).*

The Psalmist would meditate on the law of God daily. We really can do no less, but that cannot be all our relationship with God consists of. We also need the intimacy of prayer.

Intimacy can result in communication, but communication does not always result in intimacy. We see this today through our focus on the Word of God to the exclusion of prayer. We are often over-emphasizing the communication part of our relationship with God. We have promoted reading the Bible, memorizing it, and even listening to it on tapes as we are eating, driving, or even sleeping. What we end up with is Bible scholars who know the Bible from cover to cover, people who can quote huge volumes of Scripture, but who have never been prompted to develop a prayer life. The communication of Scripture has not led them to intimacy.

The Importance of Communication

In the relationship we are trying to develop with our mate or our God, communication plays a crucial role. Communication breaks down the barriers that hinder the relationship. In any relationship, including our relationship with God, we erect barriers, false fronts. We only let people go so far in knowing us and then we cut them off. We do this because we fear rejection. Most of us live with a fear that if someone knew everything there was to know about us, they would reject us. Because of that basic fear, our relationships are hindered.

Once Lou Ann and I were engaged, I felt it would be necessary for me to reveal parts of my past to her. I did not grow up in the Church as she did. Therefore we shared entirely different pasts, and I felt it would only be fair for her to make a decision regarding marriage if she knew about my past. When we would go out on a date, I would mention something I used to do. Then I would wait for her reaction. As long as I found her reaction favorable, I could reveal something else. I always waited for her reaction before I would proceed. As long as I felt she was still accepting me, even though she knew better (i.e., knew more about my past), I could reveal more things. My revelations to her were based on her acceptance of me.

The best communicating you will ever do is directly after a time of intimacy. Intimacy breaks down the barriers that hinder communication. In intimacy, everything is revealed. Knowing that all has been revealed and yet sensing an acceptance by your mate causes you to be more transparent. You don't live in fear of rejection under those circumstance.

The same is true of prayer. In prayer we are offering ourselves to God. When you come out of a time of prayer, you feel that God knows everything there is to know about you and yet He accepts you. Feeling God's acceptance of you opens your communication with God. From that sense of security, you allow the Word of God to speak to you in areas you wouldn't before. Many people struggle with letting God speak to them through His word. They fear rejection. However, they fear rejection because of the lack of intimacy between them and God.

Our biggest problem in understanding the Word of God is that we don't understand the God of the Word. Have you ever acted as a third part arbiter? You say, "What's going on here?" Person one says, "Person two said this about me." You respond by saying, "That might be what person two said, but if you knew her, you would know that is not what she meant." We determine much of what a person means by who we know them to be rather than by what they actually say. The same is true in our relationship with God. Our understanding of God's Word is heavily influenced by who we know God to be.

Yet it is only typical for the bride of Christ to put a disproportionately high priority on God's Word, the communication aspect of our relationship. Women are generally more interested in communication than they are in intimacy. It's no wonder that we, as the bride of Christ, put a high priority on studying the Scriptures, but not on prayer.

But this just isn't the way it's supposed to be. If a woman is truly interested in communication, she should give herself intimately to her husband. That would enhance communication between her and her husband quicker than anything else she could do. Similarly, if you will give yourself to God in prayer, His word comes to mean much more than it ever did before. God's Word is enhanced greatly through intimacy just as communication with your spouse is enhanced greatly through intimacy.

Submission

No book on marriage would be complete without addressing the issue of submission, a subject which has been the center of controversy in many churches. I'm not addressing submission just because I, a man, think women need to submit more. Submission is an essential element of a successful marriage, and it is simply another result of intimacy.

> *Wives, be subject [submissive] to your own husbands, as to the Lord. For the husband is the head of the wife, as Christ also is the head of the church... (Eph. 5:22,23).*

Most wives have this verse memorized because of the frequency with which it is quoted to them by their husbands. Because submission is seldom regarded outside of this context, many men (and women, too) consider submission to be a female domain. It is women who submit, not men (or so we may think). However, submission isn't just for women; it's for the whole bride of Christ, and is consequently for both husband and wife. Therefore both have equally demanding areas of submission.

The bride of Christ is in submission when she is in

prayer. The very nature of prayer is submission. The "yadah" relationship involves the hands extended in prayer. The lifted hand is symbolic of surrender. For instance, if someone sneaked up from behind you and jabbed a gun in your back, you would raise your hands; you would surrender to him.

The Wife's Submission to Her Husband

Since the wife symbolizes the Church, she submits to her husband, who symbolizes Christ. Bear in mind that the Church is always to submit to Christ. Christ never submits to the Church.

Yet some people teach and believe that there should be an "equal submission" between husband and wife. They base this upon Ephesians 5:21 which states that husband and wife should be subject to one another. At first glance, one might conclude such teachings are correct and that couples must strive for this "equal submission." However, proponents of this idea are making a serious mistake: they are yanking a sentence fragment out of Scripture and basing a teaching on it without looking at the words around it. To get a clear picture of Ephesians 5:21, you must go back to Ephesians 5:18 where the sentence begins which ends with Ephesians 5:21.

> *And do not get drunk with wine, for that is dissipation, but be filled with the Spirit, speaking to one another in psalms and hymns and spiritual songs, singing and making melody with your heart to the Lord; always giving thanks for all things in the name of our Lord Jesus Christ to God, even the Father; and be subject to one another in the fear of Christ (Eph. 5:18-21).*

Reading the verse in its context puts it in an entirely different light. These verses are directed to the entire body of Christ, both men and women. In essence they are saying, "When you come together as the bride, there should be honor preferring one another. Don't concern yourself with how much authority one person in the body may have over another. Come together to sing songs, speaking to one another in psalms and hymns and spiritual songs. Don't worry about your place of authority." As the bride of Christ, we are all equal in God's eyes.

Then the focus of Ephesians goes from the bride in general to the home. Verse 22 explains that in the home the wife submits to her husband because he represents Christ. Proposing equal submission in marriage also proposes that there be equal submission between Christ and His bride. This would mean that there are times when the Church could exercise her will over and above Christ's. It would create two heads. We wouldn't know whether the Bible or church tradition would have the final word. It would cause confusion and ultimately anarchy. You wouldn't even be able to share your faith with anybody. You might tell some that salvation is a gift of God which cannot be earned or deserved, lest any man should boast—that is what the Bible teaches. But that person could reply, "That might be what the Bible says, but my church tradition has equal authority, and it teaches that I must earn my salvation by good works."

It must be clearly understood that Christ never submits to the Church. There are instances when God answered prayers against His better judgment, but when that happened, a deep, dark emptiness entered the relationship. Psalm 106:15 says, "So He gave them their request, but sent a wasting disease [leanness into their soul] among them."

The same is true in marriage. A woman can demand her own way and get it against her husband's better judgment, but when that happens, a leanness develops in their relationship. When a woman does not honor her husband's position as Christ, a "wasting disease" will eventually destroy the home.

Demanding one's own way in either relationship paints the picture of someone praying with his hands folded while pouting and stamping his feet. Such an attitude is exactly the opposite of the "yadah" relationship of lifting our hands in surrender saying, "God, whatever you want is what I want." One of the greatest objectives of the prayer life should be getting our will lined up with God's will, not capriciously demanding our own way.

God wants the wife in total submission, just as He wants the church in total submission. The wife is to give herself unconditionally to her head. This is why traditionally the bride gives up her name during the wedding ceremony. Remember that the wedding ceremony is symbolic of salvation. The bride represents the Church, and the husband represents Christ. When a person gets saved, his identity changes, not Christ's. When I got saved, I became a Christian; Christ did not become an Auch. My identity changed. I gave up my name so I could be identified with my new husband, since we are the Bride.

There is a very anti-Christian philosophy going around which encourages women not to change their names when they get married, retaining their maiden names instead. It is even seen in the Church. For the sake of fame and fortune, some of today's Christian singers and actresses will not change their names when they marry. Where does the Bible say that certain people are exempt from certain principles? The maiden name represents you before you met Christ. After meeting Christ, the Bible says we received a new name, the old is passed away. Refusing to change your name is like saying, "I'll be a Christian, but there is no way I want to identify with Christ."

The Husband's Submission to God

As stated earlier, the husband also has an area of submission. He is to submit to God. This doesn't mean his area of submission has nothing to do with his wife. Quite the contrary — his wife is very involved.

> *Husbands, love your wives, just as Christ also loved the church and gave Himself up for her (Eph. 5:25).*

In order to submit to God, husbands must love their wives as Christ loved the Church when He sacrificed His life. The magnitude of this statement can be easily overlooked if one is not careful. God is calling for the supreme depth of love. Remember the pain and agony Jesus suffered by His own choice. Such love precludes the possibility of a husband abusing his submissive wife physically or even verbally.

However, such deep love is not common today. The amount of marital violence and the divorce statistics of our era testify to the lack of such love in contemporary marriages. In a world where such love is rare, we must look to Jesus, our model, to see where such love comes from. We should note His prayer in the Garden of Gethsemane when He said, "My Father, if it is possible, let this cup pass from Me; yet not as I will, but as Thou will" (Matt. 26:39). Jesus' great sacrifice and His love were the result of the priority God had in His life. His life was lived that God's will might be done, regardless of the personal cost. Men today will find that they will not sacrifice for their wives until pleasing the Father is their greatest objective, too. If I'm going to love my wife the way Christ loves me, I can only do that through my own love and submission to God.

It is crucial that men submit to God and seek Him earnestly, thus being able to love their wives as Christ does. A wife's submission to her husband will be a consequence of that love. So you see, if a man doesn't diligently seek God and submit to Him, he won't be able to love his wife as Christ does, and then his wife will have difficulty submitting to him.

In the natural, no man will know all the needs of his wife. Women's needs are so different from men's needs that unless the man is in tune with the Spirit of God, he will not understand what his wife's needs are. If he does not know what she needs, he cannot love her as Christ loved the Church. But being close to God makes all the difference in the world. Sometimes God will say to me, "Ron, you need to take some flowers home to your wife today." My natural reaction is, "But, God, those things will just die tomorrow. What good could they do today?" God inevitably replies, "Never mind what you think. I know what your wife needs."

So it's easy to see that only by being a man of prayer can a man truly love his wife as he should. If he isn't a man of prayer, he is giving his wife the unspoken message that he does not care enough for her to go after God's best for her.

No Overnight Miracle Cures

I hope you understand that I am not trying to introduce some type of formula whereby you can pray once, then see great things happen in your marriage overnight. What I am trying to introduce is a lifestyle of seeking God. In my experience, it was two and a half years after I had been consistently praying and seeking God that changes began to happen in our marriage, but it was well worth the wait.

I remember one occasion which took place after I had been on the road for a few weeks doing seminars and was praying about a certain matter which was requiring Lou Ann and I to make a decision. When I came back, Lou Ann and I went out to dinner. We were discussing this matter when I told her what I thought God wanted us to do. "Ron," she said, "I've told the Lord that I want to follow you in your decisions. So whatever you feel God told you to do is fine with me." It had taken her two and a half years to become comfortable with my relationship with God and for her to come to the place of really believing that God could speak to me and that I could direct the family through Him.

The Bride's Need for Security

Bill Gothard once made a statement that caught my attention. He said, "God has made the woman with a need for security, and she draws that security from her husband's relationship with God." We see the same need in the Church, Christ's bride. She draws her security from Christ's relationship with His Father. Just knowing that Jesus will never turn from His Father gives us a great sense of security. Suppose we had record of Jesus saying things like, "When it comes to God, I could take Him or leave Him," or "Sure, I love God—at least today I do." The Church would have no security in placing her salvation in the hands of Jesus if He had made such statements. However, we are very secure because we know of Christ's true relationship with His Father.

The problem most men have is they fail to realize that their wives laid down their lives for them at the wedding altar. Too many men don't have the sense to pick up that life and give them the security of a deep relationship with God. If your wife does not sense that you seek God, she will always struggle with submitting her life to you. If a woman feels insecure, she will have a tendency to try to control. I don't think that most women want to be domineering. It's just that the majority of women today are married to men that will not seek God. Those women still need security, so they find it in trying to control their situations.

Through prayerlessness, the bride of Christ is insecure today. We understand our theology. We have it in our doctrine that Jesus loves the Father, but we no longer have it in our experience. Doctrine without experience is cold, impotent, and lifeless. We have only head knowledge and a desperate need for heart knowledge. The only way to transfer head knowledge to heart knowledge is through prayer. Without knowing in our hearts that God loves us, we become very insecure. It is an insecure Church that has become militant, trying to control our world through political lobbying. Instead of salvation being our main thrust, we are seeking the salvation of our nation socially. We spend more money and time trying to correct corrupt television than we do on sharing Christ with our neighbors. It is all part of our effort to control our world because we feel insecure. The only way the Church will ever have security, though, is for the Church to go back to seeking God.

Husbands do not need to seek submission from their wives. What they really need to do is seek God—consistently and patiently. If he will submit his life to God, his wife's submission will follow.

Obedience

Sometimes people claim that they are in submission and complain that it doesn't work for them. Their problem is that they are obedient, but not submissive. When you are obedient, you have a certain set of rules and you follow them. That doesn't mean you want to, though. You may complain about those rules while you follow them. Submission, on the other hand, is having a certain set of rules and wanting to follow them. I have been obedient to many rules I was not in submission to. For example, when I was in high school, I had a curfew. I never liked that curfew. I always wanted to stay out longer. I obeyed the curfew but never submitted to it.

This doesn't mean obedience is bad. It's just that it should come as a result of submission. We should obey certain rules because we want to, because we choose to submit to them. If there's no submission before obedience, then that obedience becomes legalism. Obedience is to legalism what submission is to grace. If you go to church just because it's Sunday and not because you want to go, then your attendance does nothing to enhance your relationship with God.

I have seen many trying to hold a relationship together based on obedience. There is no submission. There's only cold, impassionate obedience. That kind of behavior won't enhance your relationship with your mate any more than legalism will enhance your relationship with God.

We live in a day of grace. We no longer live under the law. We are to first submit ourselves to God, letting obedience flow out of that. Interestingly enough, grace fulfills the law. No one can be saved through keeping the Ten Commandments, but if you are saved you will try not to break the Ten Commandments. Thus obedience flows out of submission. Our salvation fulfills the law, but the law is not what saves us. Submission changes the heart so that the heart wants to be obedient.

Obedience plays a very important role in both our marriages and our relationship with God. True obedience, obedience that comes out of submission, sharpens our spiritual hearing.

Spiritual Hearing

The apostle Paul said that marriage is a mystery (most people seem to agree with him). We need sharp spiritual hearing to understand mysteries, and this one is no exception. We sharpen our spiritual hearing through obedience to God.

> *"For nothing is hidden, except to be revealed; nor has anything been secret, but that it should come to light. If any man has ears to hear, let him hear." And He was saying to them, "Take care what you listen to. By your standard of measure it shall be measured to you; and more shall be given you besides. For whoever has, to him shall more be given; and whoever does not have, even what he has shall be taken away from him"* (Mark 4:22-25).

This verse is good news to us, faced with the mystery of marriage. Jesus said that all the mysteries of heaven will be revealed to us. However, this promise is conditional. Note the word "if." Jesus said that "if you have ears to hear," you can hear what God is saying about these mysteries. That sounds simple enough; just listen and God will tell you. But I know of more than one believer who says, "I'm listening for God and I just don't hear anything." Jesus anticipated that, so He gave us directions to sharpen our spiritual hearing.

First He said, "Take care what you listen to...." When you hear from God, be very careful because, "By your standard of measure it shall be measured to you and more shall be given to you besides." Jesus was explaining the importance of obedience. If, when you hear from God, you obey Him, then you will hear from Him again, only the next time you will hear more. Our obedience sharpens our hearing. However, disobedience dulls our hearing. If you hear a little from God, but disobey, you will have even that little taken away from you. But the choice is yours. You can choose whether or not you will listen to God. If you choose to, you can tune God out altogether. However, if we do, we dull and ultimately loose our spiritual hearing.

A Case in Point

Several years ago, a flood swept through my home town, Rapid City, South Dakota. The rain was so intense that fourteen inches had accumulated in just the first hour. Because the storm came upon the town so quickly, many people were caught unaware. Two-hundred-fifty people were drowned. However, there was one family that lived beside the creek that flooded, and they miraculously survived. When that family had first moved into their home, they made a ritual of checking the level of the creek every time it rained or stormed because they could clearly hear the waters rushing. But after a while, they got used to hearing the rushing of the water in the creek during a storm. Familiarity bred contempt, and they became convinced that the creek would never overflow. Being lulled into indifference, they stopped checking the level of the water in the creek. Through their lack or response (obedience), they dulled their hearing to the point that they would sleep through the worst storm—and they did! They slept soundly on the night when the creek overflowed and flooded the town.

The next morning when the husband woke up, he thought something looked different outside, so he went to the window. He couldn't believe what he saw—or rather what he didn't see: all his neighbors' homes were gone. He woke up his wife to tell her that not a single one of their neighbors' homes was left standing. It seemed impossible that they could have slept through anything like that. Actually they had not slept through the destruction of their neighbors' homes. In the middle of the night, the water surrounded their home and lifted it off its foundation since it was not bolted to it. Their house floated off and finally came to rest in the middle of a baseball diamond. They sat there for some time thinking everybody else had been swept away. That's dull hearing!

If you are saying, "I'll be glad to obey God, but I don't

hear Him saying anything to me," then you need to go back to the basics: the Word of God. God's Word is full of things for us to do. The Word says to pray, to witness, to be kind to the widow. If we are not doing the very basics of God's Word, how can we expect to go beyond them? Our obedience to the basics is what sharpens our hearing and through that God-will reveal the mysteries of the marriage.

I trust that at this point in the book you are beginning to see that I am not trying to introduce some kind of formula prayer that will save your marriage. I am trying to introduce a lifestyle of prayer. I am actually dealing more with you, the pray-er, than I am with the person you may be praying for. Through you own intimate relationship with God, you will communicate with Him better, your submission to Him will become what it should be, and your obedience which follows will sharpen your hearing to where God can give you the direction you need for your home.

CHAPTER NINE

Submitting To A Disobedient Husband

Those who refuse to submit to authority will be forced to submit to anarchy.
—General Robert E. Lee

Submission, as discussed in the preceding chapter, is crucial to any successful marriage. If the husband does not submit to Christ or if the wife does not submit to the husband, that marriage is in very serious danger. But is submission absolute? I've been asked by Christian women if they should submit to their husbands if their husbands are not Christians. Such husbands are not submitting to Christ, and these ladies have felt that they should not submit to them because of this. However, the husband's failure to submit to Christ does not abrogate his wife's responsibility to him. This is a very controversial topic, but I believe that as we explore God's Word in this chapter, we will see that God's Word calls for unconditional submission in order that God might be glorified.

Submission: As it Pertains to All of Us

Before looking at specific situations (such as submitting to a disobedient husband), we need to examine the general subject of submission as it applies to all of us in God's Word.

> *Submit yourselves for the Lord's sake to every human institution, whether to a king as the one in authority, or to governors as sent by him for the punishment of evildoers and the praise of those who do right. For such is the will of God that by doing right you may silence the ignorance of foolish men (1 Pet. 2:13-15).*

Peter sheds a great deal of light on the issue of submission in this portion of Scripture. To begin with, he explains that submission is "for the Lord's sake." Submission is for God's use. It's not for your use or for my use. A husband is not to submit to Christ for his own sake nor is a wife to submit to her husband out of self-interest. Submission is first and foremost a sacrifice and a service to the Lord. Secondly, we see that submission is regarded by God as "doing right." Any teachings that even hint that submission is degrading or inappropriate are just not supported by Scripture and are probably based on human pride.

> *Act as free men, and do not use your freedom as a covering for evil, but use it as bondslaves of God. Honor all men; love the brotherhood, fear God, honor the king. Servants, be submissive to your masters with all respect, not only to those who are good and gentle, but also to those who are unreasonable (1 Pet. 2:16-18).*

These are without a doubt not some of the "beloved verses" that people generally know, memorize, and quote. I think that's because these verses challenge our human nature. In the natural, we don't mind submitting to "those who are good and gentle." But, deep down in our being, we seem to recoil in horror at the thought of submitting to "those who are unreasonable." It's sort of a knee-jerk reaction. Yet God is calling us to put on the mind of Christ, not to pander to our base human nature. Therefore submission is necessary even when it rubs against our grain and inconveniences us.

> *For this finds favor, if for the sake of conscience toward God a man bears up under sorrows when suffering unjustly (1 Pet. 2:19).*

When we are suffering unjustly, we need to remind ourselves of this fact: that in so suffering we find favor with God. Because it is so contrary to our human nature and so odious to us, we must constantly remind ourselves that our suffering is a sacrifice to God, and it greatly pleases Him. Our submission is to God—then to man.

> *For what credit is there if, when you sin and are harshly treated, you endure it with patience? But if when you do what is right and suffer for it you patiently endure it, this finds favor with God (1 Pet. 2:20).*

Peter is clarifying our understanding of suffering. We seem to think that we should suffer patiently only if we have done wrong and consequently deserve to suffer. Peter turns the entire matter around and says, "What good is patient suffering when you deserve suffering?" He attributes great merit to patient suffering only when it is undeserved.

> *For you have been called for this purpose, since Christ also suffered for you, leaving you an example for you to follow in His steps, who committed no sin, nor was any deceit found in his mouth (1 Pet. 2:21,22).*

We are called to be imitators of Christ, and He is our greatest example of submission. Jesus, the sinless one, suffered and submitted to authority even though He was the only man who could have been justified by defending himself. But in order to be true imitators of Him, we must understand why He did what He did. You see, Jesus was motivated in life by one desire: to glorify the Father, not himself. That one drive caused Him to live the kind of life He lived—and to die the kind of death that He did. His motives shine out in contrast to the darkness of the motives of our natural selves, usually heavily influenced by our desire to glorify ourselves. We indulge in all kinds of posturing about our rights whenever we have been unjustly treated. To stand by and be "walked all over" is unthinkable.

> *And while being reviled, He did not revile in return; while suffering, He uttered no threats, but kept entrusting Himself to Him who judges righteously (1 Pet. 2:23).*

The power in that statement is overwhelming. Jesus didn't lash out in return, but endured the pain, entrusting himself to His Father. Jesus had His eyes fixed on eternity. But we are so unlike Him. Our gaze is consistently fixed on the present, on the injustices of the moment. Our Savior was not so short-sighted. He saw eternity, and He entrusted himself to Him who judges righteously.

> *And He Himself bore our sins in His body on the cross, that we might die to sin and live to righteousness; for by His wounds you were healed. For you were continally straying like sheep, but now you have returned to the Shepherd and Guardian of your souls (1 Pet. 2:24,25).*

As Christians we must fix our eyes on Jesus, the Author and Finisher of our faith. The last verse depicts Him in what is perhaps His greatest glory, the glory of submission. He endured the agony of the cross, unjustly accused and condemned. He suffered unjustly, in no way seeking vengeance. He submitted to the good (His Father) and to the bad, all for the sake of finding favor with His Father.

Submitting to the Disobedient

> *In the same way, you wives, be submissive to your own husbands so that even if any of them are disobedient to the word, they many be won without a word by the*

behavior of their wives (1 Pet. 3:1).

The Bible calls wives to submit to their disobedient husbands "in the same way" that Christ submitted to those who were disobedient to God (namely the polytheistic Romans and the hypocritical Jews). He submitted totally, refraining even from giving a verbal defense of himself. Why would He do this? So that ultimately He could silence their ignorance—without a word.

In spite of this clear scriptural ruling on the subject, many women struggle with the idea of submitting to a husband who is not a believer. Such wives are full of questions like, "How much do I have to submit?" "When do I submit?" and "Do I always have to submit?" If you're asking these questions, you've missed the point. If you want to be like Jesus, your goal shouldn't be submission. Instead it should be the more far-reaching goal of pleasing the Father. If your overall goal is to please Him, you won't find yourself splitting hairs over when you should submit or over how much you should submit. When your concern is pleasing and glorifying God, you will find your emphasis is on bringing your husband to salvation, not just on your submitting. That's because submission is not an end in and of itself. God has called us to submit to reach one special end: to draw others to Christ.

When people struggle with submission, it is because they are more concerned about their own welfare than they are about the welfare of others or about glorifying God. At base, they are trying to avoid unpleasantness, and, frankly, submitting is often unpleasant and painful; it was for Jesus. But God has called us to look past ourselves and look to Him and then to others.

If you are concerned about others, namely the unsaved, then you must go beyond just preaching to them, especially when dealing with an unsaved husband. That's the point Peter is making. A wife's actions will speak more loudly about Christ than her words will. This isn't to say a wife's greatest testimony to her unsaved husband is found in slavish obedience. The issue isn't her obedience. It's a matter of the wife becoming so spiritually beautiful in Christ that her husband cannot resist the Holy Spirit's work in him. Peter says that then the unsaved husbands may be won without a word "as they observe your chaste and respectful behavior" (1 Pet. 3:2).

Identifying and Removing the Threat

And let not your adornment be merely external—braiding the hair, and wearing gold jewelry, or putting on dresses; but let it be the hidden person of the heart, with the imperishable quality of a gentle and quiet spirit, which is precious in the sight of God (1 Pet. 3:3,4).

The best way to lead anybody to Christ is by showing the great change He has made in your life. If you have an unsaved husband, he needs to see more than an outward change. Since you met Christ, you may have made many outward changes. You may have quit smoking, drinking, and swearing, and those are great testimonies to what God has done in your life. But your husband needs to see more. He needs to see the hidden person of the heart. If he doesn't see that, all he sees is that your lifestyle has changed—for the worse, as far as he's concerned. You aren't interested in doing the same things you once mutually enjoyed. He begins to oppose your relationship with Christ because he sees it as something that threatens his relationship with you. He thinks, "She'll do anything for Jesus, but she won't do anything for me. She'll go to every single church function for Jesus, but she won't go anywhere with me." What's more, if a wife believes Christ should have absolute authority and denies her husband's authority as head of the house, he feels his position as head of the home is challenged, too.

I know the typical response from a Christian wife in this situation, and I can understand it. She says, "I won't go any place with him because he only wants to go to places I don't want to go to, like parties and taverns." Wife, you must realize that he wants you to go to those places because he doesn't respect your relationship with Christ. He is doing everything he can to pull you back to him because he feels like he's lost you to Jesus. You should consider that he may believe you don't love him any more.

Wife, the biggest problem you're facing right now is your husband's misconceptions about Jesus; they're the biggest obstacle to his salvation right now. He thinks Jesus has taken you from him, and he is jealous. He doesn't want to hear about the man that's stolen his wife. You need to show him that you still love him and that your new relationship with God doesn't mean you've been taken away from him. Suppose you were to go to your husband and say something like, "Honey, because of the love Jesus has given me, I love you even more now than I used to; I love you so much that I want what you want. Jesus has given me so much love for you that I want to become the kind of wife you want me to be." In time he'll begin to think, "Hey, this Jesus isn't so bad. He's actually improving my relationship with my wife."

You also need to show him that your relationship with God is not a challenge to his authority as head of the house. In short, you need to submit to your husband. You might address the issue of church attendance. He might oppose your church attendance because he doesn't understand how your going to church is doing anything but pulling you further from him. You might say, "Honey, if you don't want me to go to church, I won't. I'll only go when I have your permission." You have reaffirmed his position as head of the house.

I recall dealing with a lady in Wisconsin who had for a long time sensed her husband's disapproval about her going to church. She realized that God had instructed her to obey her husband, and that in order to obey God, she would have to obey her husband. She also realized that God could not work in her husband if she was being disobedient to Him. So she told her husband that she would only go to church if she had his permission. To her great surprise, he replied, "Your church attendance is the only thing holding our marriage together. By all means, go whenever you want to." That gave her the freedom to go whenever she wanted without feeling guilty every time she walked out the door.

This all sounds a little risky at first, but not when you grasp the principle behind it. If you will let God work through your submission, God will bring those things into your life that you desire most. In the case above, that lady turned the situation around. She reaffirmed her husband's authority over her so that her husband no longer felt threatened. Since he no longer felt threatened, he no longer needed to do anything to keep her away from church.

Entrusting Yourself to Your Father

Earlier I mentioned that Jesus entrusted himself to His Father, and that we need to follow His example. It's very important to keep this in mind because sometimes submission doesn't lead you where you want to go. It didn't lead Jesus where He wanted to go, but He prayed, "Not my will, but thine be done." Following His example, you'll need prayer to get you through.

Suppose you told your husband you wouldn't go to church unless he allowed you to and he said, "Fine. Then you're not going to church." What do you do then? The first thing you do is entrust yourself to your Father and take Him at His word. It was God who instructed you to obey your disobedient husband, so you must believe that He won't leave you stranded high and dry. He will work more quickly through your obedience to your husband (which is obedience to Him also) than He will through your disobedience. Remember that God will be working through it because it is still a matter of God allowing your husband to observe your submission.

And what about the "disaster" of being denied church attendance? This may sound strange coming from a pastor, but I don't view it as a disaster. Our primary responsibility is to be obedient to the Lord. He has ordained that you submit to your husband, and if your husband says not to go, you will be in disobedience to God if you do go after he has told you not to. This doesn't mean I discourage church attendance. Quite the contrary, I believe that when a husband and a wife are both believers, they and their family should be in church whenever the doors are open. It's just that it's a different matter entirely when the husband is not a Christian and he has forbidden his wife to go to church. The bottom line is obedience to God, so she shouldn't go.

If you struggle with submitting to your husband on this matter, consider the following questions: Does not going to church mean you will lose your salvation? Does not going to church mean you are not being obedient to God? Does not going to church mean Jesus is not Lord of your life? The answer to all these questions is "no." But would you be disobeying God by disobeying your husband? Yes, because God has commanded you to submit to him so that God might bring him salvation through your submission.

Being kept from going to church might seem like a threat to your spiritual growth, and there is potential danger there. But remember that if God asked you to be obedient to your husband (which He has), then your obedience will result in something good. You must entrust yourself to Him. God has provided the United States with virtually innumerable avenues for spiritual growth. The broadcast media is filled with Christian TV and radio programs. The recording industry releases more Christian music than you could ever buy. In addition, there are more good Christian books out there than you'll ever be able to read. But what about the children? If your husband refuses to allow you and the children to go to church, ask him if you may have devotions with the children. If he refuses that, you still have prayer! You have the ear of the God of all creation! You have the opportunity to do great spiritual things for your family through a strong prayer life!

Hope in God

For in this way in former times the holy women also, who hoped in God, used to adorn themselves, being submissive to their own husbands (1 Pet. 3:5).

Hope in God will sustain you through the trials you encounter with your husband. That's what sustained women of faith, women who believed God knew what He was talking about. Those women of old entrusted themselves to God. They were women who knew God. They were women who sought God. You can only develop their kind of hope through prayer. You will have to follow their example, praying and obeying God or you will eventually concoct your own inferior solution to your problem. If you aren't willing to spend at least one hour per day in prayer, I'm certain you will eventually go off and try to solve your problems with your husband on your own. Without prayer, your husband will never see the character of Christ in you. Your behavior just won't be what it's supposed to be if you don't pray. If, on the other hand, you do pray and seek God, His character will develop in you, and your husband will be won without a word.

Another Problem

Let's consider another problem. Suppose you tell your husband that you want what he wants, that you're willing to do as he asks. What do you do if he asks you to do something you think is wrong?

I remember talking to a woman in South Dakota who had much the same problem. Her husband said they were going to go to a bar. She stayed true to her word and went to the bar with him. That was particularly hard for her to do because he had constantly tried to get her to drink, but she always refused. By agreeing to go to the bar, she feared she was headed for conflict: to drink or not to drink? She believed drinking in the alcoholic sense was wrong, but she also believed that she should obey her husband. When they entered the bar, they were met by a good friend of the husband, and he had a big mug of beer in each hand for them. Before she could say a word, her husband stepped in front of her and firmly said, "She doesn't drink." He was protecting her. All night long he protected her from drinking. You see, drinking was not what he was trying to get his wife to do, even though he was constantly offering her a drink. He was really trying to get her to break her relationship with Christ because it threatened him. However, when his wife reaffirmed his authority over her because it was God's will, he was no longer threatened by her relationship with Him. When he realized that Christ would actually improve their marriage, he went so far as to act as his wife's protector.

I remember talking to another woman who owned a bar with her husband. When she got saved, she quit going to the bar. This threw her husband for a loop. It changed his whole life. She had always been with him at the bar to help run things, and suddenly he was alone, so he, too, saw Jesus as a threat. Finally, his wife said she would agree to tend bar if he thought it was really necessary. One day he took her up on the offer and said, "I want you to come in and work at the bar tonight." She agreed, but added, "I'm going to pray silently for everyone I serve, though." He snorted and said, "Big deal." Within two weeks, his business had dropped off so badly that he told her to go home. "If God is that upset that you're working here, I never want you to come back again." Because of her obedience, she will never need to argue with her husband about that matter again. It also demonstrates how God will take care of you when you are obedient.

Obeying God Rather Than Men

There is a very important principle we must grasp at this point. Referring back to 1 Peter 2:13,14 we read, "Submit yourselves for the Lord's sake to every human institution, whether to a king as the one in authority, or to governors as sent by Him for the punishment of evildoers and the praise of those who do right."

We are to submit to those who have authority over us, such as our local law enforcers or even the government. Since the Word of God tells us to obey the government, we have a freedom to do things which we normally could not do. That's why verse 16 says, "Act as free men, and do not use your freedom as a covering for evil."

The Bible says that we should not kill, yet in obedience to the Word we are to obey our government. Therefore, the army could send you to war and put you in the front lines where you have a direct part in killing someone, and you would not be in violation of the Scriptures. We see this all through the Old Testament where God instructed His people to go to battle even though they lived in the day of the Ten Commandments which says, "Thou shalt not kill."

Act as free men in that situation. God has given you a freedom through your submission to those in authority over you to do something that under other circumstances would be considered evil. In obedience to your government (in a war-type situation) killing the enemy is not morally wrong. However, if an army officer were to ask you to kill your neighbor, that would be morally wrong (because you are going against the laws of your society) and you would be using your freedom as a covering for evil.

God has asked the wife to be obedient to a disobedient husband. Therefore, your obedience to him is not morally wrong. However, if he asked you to do something morally wrong you must obey God rather than man.

In Acts 5:29, Peter was driven to the point where he said, "We must obey God rather than men." Just as was true for Peter, so also for us there are times when we must obey God rather than men. God has commanded you to obey your husband, but you shouldn't if he insists that you do something immoral. You mustn't sin if your husband tells you to. For the ladies in the stories I've described, going to a bar was not immoral; only drinking was. But because of divine principle and because they continued to entrust themselves to God, they were not confronted with such a moral conflict. Bear in mind that Jesus went to that era's social equivalent of bars—only to bring people back out with Him.

Righteousness

For the eyes of the Lord are upon the righteous, and His

ears attend to their prayer... (1 Pet. 3:12).

We know how necessary prayer is, and so we want God to hear our prayers. This verse tells us that He listens to the prayers of the righteous and that He watches over them. That makes being righteous very important. Unfortunately, many people today don't really understand what righteousness is. Some confuse it with godliness, which deals with our relationship with God. Righteousness, on the other hand, deals with our godly treatment of others. Jesus summed up the whole of righteousness by giving us what has become known as the golden rule: "Do unto others as you would have them do unto you."

If you want God to hear and answer your prayers for your husband, you're going to have to be careful to put the golden rule into effect in your life. And it's not conditional. It doesn't say "If people are nice to you, then do unto them as you would have them do unto you." It applies to every one or it means nothing. God hears the prayers of those who treat people the way God does, not those who return evil for evil. The face of the Lord is against those who do evil.

The history of mankind, watered by a small ocean of blood as it is, demonstrates clearly the difficulty we have with putting this into practice. It proves nobody can do it by himself. You need God to help you treat your spouse this way. As you consistently spend time in God's presence, you will begin to sense God speaking to you, just as surely as you speak to Him. He will begin to give you insight into your mate. There is nothing He doesn't know about your spouse, so you can count on Him to help you out in this area.

Facing Criticism

But even if you should suffer for the sake of righteousness, you are blessed. And do not fear their intimidation, and do not be troubled, but sanctify Christ as Lord in your hearts, always being ready to make a defense to everyone who asks you to give an account for the hope that is in you, yet with gentleness and reverence (1 Pet. 3:14,15).

You can expect people to criticize you for your obedience to a disobedient husband. In order to face this, you must sanctify Christ as Lord in your heart. You must make the determination that you are submitting to your husband because it is Jesus' will and because He is the Lord of your life. That becomes your defense to everyone who asks you to give an account of your actions.

And keeps a good conscience so that in the thing in which you are slandered, those who revile your good behavior in Christ may be put to shame (1 Pet. 3:16).

You may be criticized by people today, but your critics will be put to shame the day you walk into church hand in hand with your husband. Then you will see that the criticism of man is foolishness when compared with the faithfulness of God.

Who once were disobedient, when the patience of God kept waiting in the days of Noah, during the construction of the ark, in which a few, that is, eight persons, were brought safely through the water (1 Pet. 3:20).

Noah was criticized for his obedience to God, just as every prophet who followed him was. But Noah determined in his heart that he was going to obey God, regardless of what people around him thought. Plank by plank, year after year, he labored on the ark while his neighbors hurled insults and laughed at him. He resolved that he would be obedient to God no matter what happened and through that his critics were silenced and his family was saved.

CHAPTER TEN

Developing Godliness

*It is our lack of godliness that has brought us all to the
very brink of disaster.*
—William Lloyd Garrison

Most Christians agree that God is the answer to all
problems. Yet most Christians with problems are not seeking
God. Instead they are just seeking answers to their problems.
They are obsessed with finding resolutions to the conflicts in
their lives, but have little time for pursuing their God. Their
quest for answers is so tragic because it is so vain. Answers
are not the answer they need; God is. This may sound
contradictory, but it isn't.

I can remember when I was a little boy learning how to
ride my bike. Like most boys and girls my age, I often fell off,
suffering my share of scrapes and bruises (at the time it
seemed like more than my share). I would run into the house,
tears streaming down my face, looking for my mom. She
applied the necessary first-aid, but that wasn't what I really
came in the house for. I came in for her to "kiss it and make
it all better." I ran to her so she could put her arms around me
and comfort me. At that moment, I had a greater need for my
mom than for any of her ministrations. Even if she could have

miraculously made my sore disappear, I still would have been looking for more. I would still have been looking for the comfort and love of my mom. But as adults we seem to change.

No matter how old we get, we still experience pain. Just as it was during childhood, pain is still part of life. The difference is that, as adults, all we seek is first-aid, the "practical" alleviation of our sorrows. We reason that the problem we face caused the pain in the first place, so to get rid of the pain, all we need to do is get rid of the problem. Guided by this sort of reasoning, we become preoccupied with searching for a way to remove our problem and with it our pain. In so doing, we neglect our need to feel our spiritual parent's arms around us to comfort us. When we have a problem that rivets us with despair, we need God's comfort every bit as much as we need that problem to be resolved. In fact we may need that interaction with God even more than we need for our problem to be eliminated. We are diligently endeavoring to find a bandage and some antiseptic solution for our "owie," but we really need more than that.

Our greatest problem is that as adults we keep falling off our "bike." Just as when we were children, first-aid will not keep us on our bike. But, unlike our childhood experiences, we cannot learn to stay on the bike by just sticking with it. As we approach the broad, serious issues of life, we need God to teach us how to ride without getting hurt. He is the only one who can do it. Yet we only appeal to God after the fact, after we are suffering from some problem, after we have fallen off our bike. We seek a bandage, and that's all. We should really be trying to prevent these problems from occurring at all. We need to ask God to teach us how to ride the bike so that we won't fall off and have any need for a bandage.

What God longs to teach us is godliness. We suffer from a devastating lack of godliness and live with all kinds of problems and all kinds of hurts as a result. But if we will allow God to teach us godliness, the development of that godliness within us will solve most of the problems we face. Any time we seek anything from God, we must be involved in prayer.

It must be clearly understood at the outset that prayer is no guarantee that your spouse will be changed, however, it's just that we have no other option. Prayer is the most powerful thing we have, it's just that even prayer cannot force a man's will. Therefore the pray-er must change their own will. The catch, if you will, is that its most powerful results occur in the person praying rather than in the person being prayed for. Through prayer, you are submitting your will to God. Then God can take you, a willing vessel, and make you into what He wants you to be, using you to change the person you are praying for.

Flowers Can't Change Your Marriage

Many marriage seminars and retreats expend themselves with teachings about all the things you can do to make your spouse happy. They suggest sending flowers, writing little love notes, going out to dinner, and so on. These nice little romantic gestures promise grand, sweeping changes, but produce only temporary relief. They cannot offer a lasting solution to a troubled situation. Teachings that limit themselves to these marital niceties bypass the real key to happiness in the home because they neglect the need for us to develop the character of God.

Little romantic gimmicks can't really improve your marriage because they presuppose that your love for your spouse is based on what he or she does. In reality, true, solid, lasting love for your mate must be based on who that person is, not just on the things he or she does. If you try improving your marriage just by doing these things without changing your character, you will be sadly disappointed. That's what I discovered early in my marriage.

When Lou Ann and I were first married, I was still attending Bible college while also serving as an associate pastor at a local church. Needless to say, times were tough and money was in short supply. On one particularly turbulent morning, Lou Ann and I had an intense argument over the state of our finances. It left me with an unsettled feeling all day. I wanted desperately to reconcile myself with her, but I wasn't sure what to do. Then it hit me! On my way home from church, I would stop and buy her some flowers. A man once said that there is no problem a man can have with his wife that he can't solve with a bouquet of flowers (that man was a florist who had been divorced three times). As I walked through the door with my peace offering, I struggled to suppress a grin. I knew she was about to melt all over me. But when she saw those flowers, she was furious. She couldn't believe I was so thoughtless. As it was, we never had enough money for anything, and I had just spent what little we did have on useless flowers, she said.

Things don't solve problems, only changed character does. I am not opposed to nice romantic gestures. I do believe, however, that those things should be the result of who God is turning us into. They should not be the result of trying to cover up who we really are. In my marriage, I have found that real happiness began when my wife started perceiving how God was changing me. Now when I bring flowers to my wife or do something like that, it is because of who God has made me, not because I'm trying to cover up something I've done or something I am.

Great Expectations

Perhaps one of the greatest problems in marriages today is that we require our mates to meet our unreasonably high expectations of them. When we married them, we assumed they would meet our expectations. When we see they are unable to, we realize that we had a false perception of them. They don't seem like the people we dated and walked down the aisle with. Depression descends like a gray, dismal mist, and arguments begin. Statements like, "You're not the man I married!" and "You're so different from when we were dating!" are made with regularity because they don't meet the high standards we set for them.

Great expectations are a healthy ingredient in one's life, but they must not be directed at one's spouse. High expectations for your spouse are usually an indication that you are depending on that person for your happiness. Actually your expectations should be aimed at God. If you expect God to be everything the Bible says He is, you will never be disappointed or depressed by Him. The Lord should always be your basis for happiness. If your happiness is based on who God is, you will never have a reason for depression.

My soul, wait in silence for God only, for my hope is from Him (Ps. 62:5).

The Psalmist agreed that our only hope should come from God. The inference is that we should not truly hope in anyone else or develop expectations of somebody besides God. But before we can really develop expectations of God, we must have a great sense of dependency on Him and begin to trust Him. This brings us back to prayer because only in prayer do we develop dependency on God. You see, as we persevere in prayer, we slowly but steadily get to know God. As we begin to get to know Him, we begin to trust Him. But until you really get to know Him, you will always find it difficult to trust Him.

One of the greatest problems in modern Christianity is that God's people struggle with trusting Him. Even though we know that He is God, we have a hard time trusting Him because we lack intimate (yadah) relationship with Him. Preachers are telling their congregations, "Just trust God! That's all there is to it!" And to an extent, they are giving their people the right direction. We all do need to trust God. But this kind of advice is useless until we know God. We cannot trust someone we do not know. So we end up praying things like, "God, I'm turning this problem over to you completely. I wash my hands of the whole thing. It's your problem now. However, I do reserve the right to worry about it. And I'd like to worry about it a lot. See, in case You don't come through, I will have worried about it, and that should help quite a bit." That's the kind of prayer every believer will pray until he knows God, because until then, he won't be able to trust Him.

If, on the other hand, we do grow to know and trust God, we will develop realistic expectations of Him. When problems come along, we will expect God to take care of them as we are faithful to Him and continue to pray. Most Christians today can't say that they do that. Most don't expect God to make a difference in their homes. That is just a natural result of not spending time in God's presence.

One of the key reasons people don't generally expect God to make a difference is that they have a guilty conscience. They know they should spend more time with God, but they don't. Inwardly, they think, "I haven't done my part in my relationship with God, so why should God do His part?" Please understand that this is a problem we're having, not a problem God is having. God is far more faithful to us than we are to Him. It's just that we have a problem with trusting God because we don't pray. We don't expect God to help, so our expectations are all directed toward our mates. Subsequently, all the happiness of our home is based on our mates.

Ladies, suppose that you are married to a man who never compliments anything you do, so you determine that you are going to have everything so perfect when he comes home that he will have to recognize your efforts. The house is clean (you had someone from the agency come in to clean it). The children are quiet (they're at the neighbors'). Dinner is flawless (you had it catered). Your husband comes home, takes off his shoes, turns on the TV, and never even notices how clean the house is. He's even able to take a short nap before dinner because there are no noisy kids. He gets up for dinner and eats everything on his plate—twice—because it's so good. But he never says a word to you about the extra time that must have been required to make things look so nice. If your expectations gravitate around him, you would be very disappointed. If your expectations come from God, then there is no need whatsoever to be disappointed.

Invariably when our expectations come from others, and they don't react the way we anticipated, we throw up our hands in disgust and say, "What's the use? I've tired everything and nothing makes a difference." Part of the problem is that you've tried everything except praying and giving the situation to God. If you really desire to achieve success, you must pray. If you do not pray, you are left with trying to force changes into existence yourself. If you aren't really seeking God, then you put most of your hope or expectation into what you are doing in an effort to make a difference in your home. If your hope is in what you are doing, then all your expectations will be based in how others react to what you are doing. Their reactions will become the barometer of your success. If they didn't reacted the way you wanted them to, all your hopes are dashed because they were based exclusively on those reactions. With this in mind, it is easy to see that God must become the hope of your home.

The Hope of the Home

How does God actually bring us to the place of expecting from Him rather than from others? First, you must understand that expectation is synonymous with hope. The two can be used interchangeably. Second, we must see how hope or expectation is developed. To many, this might come as a surprise, but hope is developed through tribulation.

> *And not only this, but we also exult in our tribulations, knowing that tribulation brings about perseverance; and perseverance, proven character; and proven character, hope; and hope does not disappoint, because the love of God has been poured out within our hearts through the Holy Spirit who was given to us (Rom. 5:3-5).*

Since tribulation is the basis for hope, some of you have some very hopeful situations. But this doesn't mean tribulation automatically results in hope. If it were automatic, you'd have it made. The more you fight, producing tribulation, the better off you'd be because your hope would be proportional to your tribulation. That is simply not the case, though.

When your mate doesn't live up to your expectations of him or her, tribulation generally follows. However, tribulation does not automatically produce hope; tribulation produces prayer. Therefore, that which tribulation produces (namely, prayer) yields hope. Tribulation is always meant to bring us to prayer.

> *Do not hide Thy face from me in the day of my distress...*
> *(Ps. 102:2).*

King David's many tribulations drove him to God. He knew the distress of military defeat, moral decay, and a disobedient son who attempted a coup of his government. In his distress, David sought God. Yet many of us fail to follow his example. When we are faced with tribulations, fights, and misunderstandings in our marriages, we seek to solve these problems without praying. Ironically, those problems are part of the natural process God is taking us through in order to get us to pray. If we would allow our maturity in Christ to draw us to prayer, we could avoid most of the trials of life. Unfortunately, we usually wait until things are unbearably bad before we will pray. If that continues to be our tendency, trials and tests will always be a part of life.

God tells us in His Word that once He begins a good work in us, He will bring it through to maturity. We can rest assured that God is not going to give up on the development of His character in us. If we will not seek God on our own, then tribulation will drive us to it. God will allow trying circumstances in our lives to push us to prayer, which, in turn, develops God's character in us.

The problem in most marriages is a lack of God's character. That deficiency prevents husbands and wives from getting along with each other. Do you think the Father and Jesus argue over matters as trivial as squeezing the toothpaste tube in the middle or rolling it up from the end? Although we can consider it a moot point since we assume they don't brush, it would be absurd to think that such inconsequential issues would taint their relationship. If that is the case with Jesus and His Father, then why isn't it the case with you and your mate? Why do such things cause arguments between two people? It is because they lack the character of

God. Consider also that if such trivial concerns hamper your relationship with your spouse, what will happen when you really have something to argue about?

Hope Does Not Disappoint

Looking back at Romans 5:5, we read, "Hope does not disappoint, because the love of God has been poured out within our hearts...." Paul told his Roman readers first that hope would not disappoint them. Then he told them how it works: by God's love being poured into our hearts. You see, if you come to the realization that you cannot change your mate, then you turn responsibility for changing that person over to God. If you then see that God is working in your mate, you no longer have to be upset over who they are. How can you hold anything against your mate that God has not yet brought into his or her life? If God is the one who brings about change, and God has not yet changed your mate, you cannot blame that person for being a certain way. The primary reason for someone not changing is us not praying.

It is only from a lack of prayer that you see through man's eyes rather than God's. When you begin praying for someone, in this case your mate, you start seeing that person the way God does. You start to love your spouse as God does: for who that person is, rather than for what he or she does. Hope does not disappoint us because God's love is poured out in our hearts. Prayer changes the pray-er. It takes the pray-er from brotherly love (called "phileo" in Greek) to godly love (the Greek "agape"). Every human has a certain natural capacity for love, even the most ungodly of men. What we must do is move from that natural ability to love into God's ability to love. We are glad that God loves us with all our flaws and inadequacies, but we usually don't want to love others until they are perfect. God wants us to love others the way He loves us. That can only happen when we develop His character in us, and that requires time in His presence.

But you can't pray for this "agape" love. It only comes as a result of being with God. He doesn't dump it out in bulk quantities to whoever asks for it. The Scriptures say, "God is love, and he who does not love does not know God." It doesn't say, "He who does not love needs more love." It says he doesn't know God; that's the main problem, the lack of love is only a symptom of the real problem. If I regularly spend time in God's presence, I won't be able to help loving everyone, even the most unlovely person. But if I leave God's presence for even a small march of days or weeks, I will love only conditionally. If someone meets a certain criteria, I will love that person to pieces. But if they don't measure up, I won't, all because I haven't been in God's presence.

That's why I said earlier that God is using your present situation, no matter how bad it is, to develop His character in you, if you will just let it drive you to prayer. If it doesn't drive you to prayer, then things will probably never change for you. You will have to live with those same problems every day for the rest of your life here on earth.

All this talk about praying for our spouses may make them seem bad, but remember that God uses what naturally interests us (like our mate, family) to get us to pray so that He can supernaturally change us. The change must happen in us first. God has to first get me to the place where I can love others the way He loves me. Then He can begin to work through my prayers for them and begin to change my spouse.

If God could instill this hope in every one of us, we'd slash the divorce rate to a mere fraction of its current size. A survey I saw a couple years ago indicated that the annual divorce rate was around seventy-five percent. That means three out of every four marriages end in divorce. Dr. Richard Dobbins' organization performed another study analyzing divorce within the Church. They found that where couples that attend church regularly are concerned, only one out of every fifty marriages ended in divorce. That's still one too many in every fifty marriages, and we'd like to see better, but at least that's a better statistic than the world is offering us. The survey of church people was taken a bit farther, getting more specific. They studied families that pray together. They found that in such marriages only one in every eleven hundred marriages ends in divorce. This is because prayer generates an awareness of God, and in God's presence men flee from iniquity. Too many of our Christian homes are not living in the presence of God and, subsequently, we involve ourselves in many activities we would not if we were aware of God's presence. So when we face tribulation, we go to prayer. Prayer causes us to spend time in God's presence, and that causes us to become like Him in character, which in turn causes us to have great hope in even the most devastating situation.

Don't Give Up on Your Spouse

Paul said in his letter to the Romans that God caused Israel to stumble, giving her a spirit of stupor, eyes to see not and ears to hear not so she would reject the gospel. So then the question was asked, "Did God cause Israel to fall so as to be lost forever?"

I say then, they did not stumble so as to fall, did they? May it never be! But by their transgression salvation has come to the Gentiles, to make them jealous (Rom. 11:11).

Israel is God's spiritual wife. Out of the intimate relationship between God and Israel, a spiritual Son was born: Jesus. However, as His wife, Israel rejected Him. In a certain spiritual sense, God is separated from His spouse because she has deserted Him. As a result, He has put all of His attention on His Son, through whom we can have a relationship with God. According to the Scripture this has happened in order to provoke Israel, His wife, back to Him through jealousy. God is working on getting His wife back; He's not giving up on her. He doesn't believe in divorce and neither should we.

We need to address the issue of divorce, but before we do, I want to preface that discussion with a few words. The only reason I want to address divorce is to keep it from happening, not to condemn those who have already gone through it. I have no wish to condemn the past, only to preserve the present and help save the future. In fact, I think most divorced people would be the first to be on my side because they, too, would want to prevent someone from going through what they went through. That is the spirit in which I present this. It's against divorce, but not against the divorcee. God is in the business of turning your life into something that will please Him regardless of what you've been through.

Because God won't divorce Israel (and He has more than just cause to do so), we Christians must be just as opposed to divorce. I understand that there are situations when divorce can be thrust upon you, when your mate is resolute and determined to seek divorce. However, I believe a Christian should never initiate divorce proceedings. Remember that God's wife has left Him, but He has not and will not give up on His wayward wife. He is doing all He can to woo her back to Him. God will never ask us to go through something He has never gone through. You may say, "It's easy for you to say all this about sticking it out, but you don't know what I'm going through." That's right, I don't but God does because He's gone through it.

Understand what this means, though. God will never offer solution without sacrifice. That is how He remedied our problem with the wages of our sin. To offer a solution without sacrifice is ungodly. The only solution God ever offers us is through His own sacrifice. I learned this lesson many years ago.

While I was attending Bible college I worked at an office in the Sears department store chain. It gave me an opportunity to use the computer degree I earned at a business college before I was saved. My job was a bitter sweet one: I generated the local payroll. Some of the pay checks that rolled off the computer printer were just plain amazing to me at the time. Some executives took home monthly checks for as much as $70,000. Then I would see mine advancing from the same printer just behind those; it was for a meager $125. Sometimes I felt sorry for myself. As I watched the checks printing on that long sheet, I would say, "God, here I am, a poor college student. I obviously need this money more than these people do." I might even throw in an occasional "Woe is me." Then one day I was reading my Bible, and a certain verse caught my attention. It seemed to be addressed to me personally.

> *Slaves, be obedient to those who are your master according to the flesh, with fear and trembling, in the sincerity of your heart, as to Christ; not by way of eyeservice, as men-pleasers, but as slaves of Christ, doing the will of God from the heart (Eph. 6:5,6).*

As I read that, God began to say, "Ron, you need to die to self. Your problem is that self is getting in the way, and you're thinking of doing service to man instead of to Me." Do you know why He could say, "Die to self?" Because long before He ever told me to do it, Jesus died. His solution for my problem comes through His sacrifice. If God's solution to you is to hang in there, it's because that's what He is doing.

Rights and Responsibilities

In the United States, we are far more rights conscious than responsibilities conscious. We go charging after our rights, and throw our responsibilities aside. Do you know that you may have someone dead to rights with a biblical basis for divorce, but over and above your rights, you have a responsibility? I believe that responsibility outweighs our rights. That's why I don't deal with the question of when you should and shouldn't get a divorce. I don't think you should get a divorce. In Matthew 19, when Jesus was asked about divorce, He said it was wrong, that in the beginning it was never meant to be. He said Moses permitted the children of Israel to divorce only because of the hardness of their hearts. That's what's really behind divorce: hard hearts. They are hearts which are more concerned with what they have a right to than they are with what their responsibilities are.

We need to wake up to the reality that God has every one of us dead to rights. None of us deserve salvation. But God overlooked His own rights. He looked at the responsibility He had to His own Son and has granted to us what we have no right to. I remember talking to a woman with a very sad marital situation. Her husband was an alcoholic, and her life was actually in danger. She mentioned that a few years earlier, he had an affair. I asked if she was going to use that as a basis to pursue a divorce. She looked at me rather strangely and said, "Heavens no! When that happened, I forgave him of it, and that's settled. Since I've forgiven him, I haven't got a right to use it against him." I felt like Jesus must have when He saw the face of the centurion. I felt like saying, "In all the land, I have not seen such faith." I hadn't seen such a practical application of Christianity in years. Can you imagine just forgiving someone? We seem so unwilling to do that. We'd be more inclined to say, "Now I've got him! Away with him." We seize our rights, but we neglect our responsibility to forgive.

The husband's main objective in life is to offer up to Jesus a bride without spot or wrinkle. Christ, too, is preparing a Bride. He gives all His attention to the preparation of His bride. One day He will offer up to His Father His bride without spot or wrinkle. One day, men, we will also stand before God and say, "Here, Father, is what I've done with what you've entrusted to me." Men, if you're going to do that, you must give up your rights. You have a responsibility to God and to your family. In order for me to help my family develop in the things of God, I have had to give up all of my rights—but how much did Jesus love the Church? So much that He gave himself to it and died for it. Rest assured that no reward will ever surpass the joy of seeing your entire family standing before God.

Do you know why the man's primary goal in life is the spiritual development of his family? Because God is going to draw Israel back to Him through provoking her to jealousy. This is why Jesus gives all His attention to the Church: if the Church was fully developed and fully mature, then the whole world would be jealous of the relationship we have with God. When our families are fully developed in the things of God, they will become a very powerful and effective evangelistic tool because this world has sought every means to save their families. The world has tried everything from psychology to mysticism, and none of it has worked. In fact, things are only growing worse. And only the church has the answer: a relationship with Jesus Christ. The world should be literally breaking down the doors of the church saying, "We've noticed that your families have what we seek." If we would give ourselves to the developing of our families, it would be a tremendous force for completing the Great Commission.

We have a responsibility to God, to our families, and to the world to reflect the glory of Jesus Christ.

CHAPTER ELEVEN

A Spotless Bride

Every man will proclaim his own love, but who can find a faithful man?
—King Solomon

Several years ago I lived next door to a fanatical golf enthusiast. He lived, breathed, ate, and slept golf. No matter where he went—on vacation or on business trips—he took his clubs with him. When he wasn't playing golf, he was watching a tournament on television. He always boasted that his greatest goal in life was to play a round of golf in every state in the U.S. (which led him and his reluctant wife to some vacations in states which offered little more for a vacation than a golf course in a new state). Although I have nothing against a hobby or a sport, I think they can be problems when our greatest objectives in life revolve around them.

As a Christian, the husband's main objective in life should be to offer his wife to God without spot or wrinkle. Remember, men, you represent Christ in the marriage, and your wife and family represent the Church, the bride of Christ. You must imitate Jesus who is presently giving all of His attention to the development of His bride. And why is He giving so much attention to His bride? Ephesians 5:27 tells us

Christ is giving so much attention to His bride in order "that He might present to Himself the church in all her glory, having no spot or wrinkle or any such thing; but that she should be holy and blameless."

Christ's thoughts and energies are focused on His church in all her glory. One day He will stand before the Father and present His bride to Him. One day, husband, you will stand before the Father and say, "Father, here is what I have done with what you have given me—here is my bride." Will she be without spot or wrinkle? Will all of your children stand in heaven with you?

A World Scarred by Faithlessness

Let's consider Hebrews 3:6 for a moment. "But Christ was faithful as a Son over His house whose house we are...." Christ was appointed over the Church and was found faithful. However in Hebrews 3:2 it says, "He was faithful to Him who appointed Him...." Jesus was faithful to His father. Jesus was a faithful son. I have a great concern that our fathers today are no longer faithful to God. Subsequently the home suffers. A father's commitment to his home is just as important as Christ's commitment to the Church. What would have happened if Christ suddenly decided to abandon the Church?

My youngest brother, Darryl, used to live in St. Paul, Minnesota. He and his family lived in the only house on his block. The rest of the block was full of apartments. His was the only single family dwelling on the block. Their daughter, Sarah, was playing out in their back yard one day when several of the other girls from the neighborhood came and began to question her about living in the big house while they all lived in the apartments. They began to ask her who all lived in there with her. She said, "My mommy and daddy and brother." This seemed to surprise the other girls and they said, "You mean that your mommy and daddy live in the same house?" Each of those girls came from broken homes and thought it odd that a child would live with both parents. That is a sad commentary on our society today. Where are the faithful fathers?

Proverbs 17:6 states, "...And the glory of sons [children] is their fathers." An increasing number of children in our society have no father, at least not in the conventional sense, and they are loosing out. They are being deprived of the glory of having a father. They either have no father at home or they have a father who is not faithful to God. We have fathers that are more concerned with making it rich than offering their families up to God. Unfortunately for our families, we focus more on what God wants to give us than on what we should give God. The rejected children are hurt emotionally and even physically as their self-absorbed mom and dad concentrate on being successful.

We have a generation of self-preoccupied parents who do little more for their children than spout "statements of faith." Preachers have pandered to their selfish lifestyles by telling them, "Your kid will make it if you have enough faith" and "All you need to do is claim your child's salvation and then you can get back to focusing on your needs." There is more to being a parent than just claiming your child's salvation. Doing that only is just the advice selfish parents want to hear because they are not willing to invest any more of their precious time in their children. I thank God that Jesus didn't just claim our salvation and then abandon us.

My first week as a youth pastor turned out to be a week I'll never forget. On my first Saturday, we conducted a funeral for a fourteen-year-old girl from our group who died from an unknown disease. It came as a complete shock. Just two weeks earlier she was healthy and happy. Then one day she became ill, so her parents took her to the doctor. The doctor immediately sent her to the hospital where she died. A couple of months after the funeral, her father came to me and said, "For years God has been trying to get my attention and I would not listen. My goal in life was to be a material success. That's where my heart was, that's the only thing I paid any attention to. Today—finally—God has my attention. Oh how I wish I had listened to Him before I had to sacrifice."

Our children in the U.S. are suffering terribly as a result of faithless fathers. In his book, *America's Last Frontier*, Bill Wilson, who has established a ministry to children in the ghettos of New York City, graphically illustrates this fact. He writes, "I was standing in the dark hallway talking to an eight year old. The only light in this fourth floor of the tenement came from the skylight in the roof. There was just enough light to see her face as she spoke. 'I'm the only one with my own father,' she blurted out nonchalantly. At first I didn't think anything of it, but then my curiosity was aroused. I'd been in the ghetto long enough to know when to ask questions and when to remain silent, so I looked at her and asked, 'What do you mean by that?' 'Well, my two older brothers have their father, my younger brother and sister have their father, and the two babies have their father, I'm the only one with my own father.' I realized exactly what she meant: her mother had seven children by four different men and she shared no brothers and sisters with her father. How pitiful, how sinful, and this eight-year-old girl has no idea of the wrongness of her mother's actions. Unless the chain is broken, this little girl will grow up and live just like her mother."

Self-Denial

Although He was a Son, He learned obedience from the things which He suffered (Heb. 5:8).

Jesus, the faithful Son of God, learned to be obedient through the things he suffered. This is not referring to the suffering of the Cross, but rather it's a reference to the suffering that comes through self-denial. Jesus Christ denied himself in order to become the source of eternal salvation. Likewise, a father's faithfulness to God points out the way of salvation for his children. It is no simple thing to be a father. Jesus died to self so that we might live. Fathers must die to self so their families might live.

The wife may be the heart of the home, but the husband is to be its spiritual head. If you are not a man of prayer, you are not setting an example before your children that will build strong Christians.

After teaching on prayer in a certain church one evening, the pastor got up and confessed to his congregation that there was a time when he did not pray with his children. He admitted that he had not been opposed to it, but that he had simply been indifferent to it. He had been content with his wife doing it. Then he told us how his attitude was changed one day when he and his family were driving home from vacation. The children were asleep in the back seat when his wife pointedly said, "You need to start praying with your children when they go to bed at night. I've noticed that our daughter can pray up a storm, but your son doesn't understand the first thing about prayer." He quickly realized that he was not setting an example his own son could live by.

Christ loved His bride so much that He died for her. Do you love your bride (family) enough to die to self in pursuit of God? Will you die to the desires of the flesh and pull yourself out of bed on behalf of your family? When all the rest of life passes by, the only thing that will stand will be your family's relationship with God. The only thing that will matter to you will be that your family knows God, that your family spends eternity in heaven. Will you and I offer up to Jesus a bride without spot or wrinkle?

CHAPTER TWELVE

But Now Abide

But now abide faith, hope, love, these three; but the
greatest of these is love (1 Cor. 13:13).

God takes our marriages through several stages in order
to develop His character in us. The first stage, faith, is one all
married couples can look back on with fondness. When my
wife and I were first married, we had a great deal of faith in
our relationship. Ours was to be the marriage without conflict or incident of any kind. I remember how optimistic I was
when we were going through premarital counseling. I smiled
the obligatory smile and nodded at the proper intervals, but
as I listened to the pastor, I was sure we had no need for his
advice. He didn't understand like I did that our marriage was
going to be perfect; it wasn't going to be like all those others
he had witnessed.

I had a lot of faith that everything was going to be fine,
but faith is not enough. In order to help us to continue to
develop in His character, God helps us to add hope to our
faith. Unfortunately for us, hope comes only through tribulation, and none of us wants to experience tribulation, especially in our marriage. Yet when the honeymoon is over, we
find out just what we got ourselves into, and we must all face

some level of tribulation. However, tribulation is a very good thing because it draws us to God and pushes us toward prayer. We see how terrible things look, but we also hope in God. As we pray, God continues to work on us to shape us into His likeness. Our faithfulness in prayer generates love within us, the very character of God. Out of all three, faith, hope, and love, the last, love, is the greatest.

Lacking Love

Even though God's Word extols love as the greatest of the three, popular preaching seems to disagree. Many pastors and evangelists place a great emphasis on faith, but are strangely silent about love. In Jesus' ministry, faith and love were inseparable.

> And a leper came to Him, beseeching Him and falling on his knees before Him, and saying to Him, "If You are willing, You can make me clean." And moved with compassion, He stretched out His hand, and touched him, and said to him, "I am willing; be cleansed." And immediately the leprosy left him and he was cleansed (Mark 1:40-42).

Compassion should be the catalyst for faith. When it is not, the end result is invariably pride. Jesus never demonstrated pride, but healed many because He was compelled by compassion. We experience this when we are faced with a loved one near death. Our great love for that person causes us to pray with more faith. It is during those times that we desperately cry out to God. It is during those times that we determine not to stop praying until we have faith for the fruit of the Spirit in his life.

Often an evangelist, especially if he is televised, is greatly revered because of his excellent preaching. Some believers get the idea that God begins His day by checking in with that preacher. Then believers catch him in a situation where he is rude, obstinate, or even vulgar, anything but compassionate, and their great hope is crushed. Some are then so devastated that they begin to wonder whether anything about Christianity is real. The mistake they make is that they are unduly swayed by a man's God-given abilities. His abilities are not nearly as important as having love, joy, peace, and so on. Those traits are what will prove the real value of his ministry. When you hear a preacher, you should ask yourself, "Has this man developed the character of God?" If he does not have love, he is nothing.

When a preacher lacks love, he is in trouble. The man who takes great steps of faith or who has great natural talents is in the worst predicament if he lacks love. Such a man will become intensely proud of how God is using him. Frequently God uses such a man in great ways, but that individual will not give God the glory for it because his character is so impoverished. His pride will lead him to take the praise that rightly belongs to God. This kind of person really can't help himself. Since he hasn't developed God-like character, he will naturally swell with pride. Without God's character, he has no choice in the matter.

The lack of prayer invariably results in pride. However, if you pray, you will develop a great capacity to love. When you spend time in the presence of God regularly, you can't help loving those around you more.

In the Evangelical world, there is much teaching about faith. However, some people who spend little or no time with God have learned how to exercise their faith. They find they are doing things for God, but lack character development. When you add a lack of character to great achievements, you always end up with pride. Worse yet, we have ended up with "men of faith," men who preach a faith message, but who have very little compassion. That deficiency causes their message to come across in a very condemning manner. In fact, I know of one specific word used by several men to describe people who do not understand or do not agree with their message: "stupid." On numerous occasions, I have heard "men of faith" castigate fellow believers as being stupid just because they don't understand their message or don't agree with it. Such statements have nothing to do with compassion. Can you imagine Jesus sneering, "You're stupid!" at someone? Did you ever notice the following Scripture in the Bible? "And Jesus, being moved with compassion, reached out His hand and cried, 'You are all stupid! You haven't received that which is yours!'" You've never seen such a Scripture because none exists, nothing even close to it.

Many men boast about their faith, and perhaps they do have great faith. But Paul said that out of faith, hope, and love, love is the greatest. The development of God's character is the greatest, and that character is saturated with love.

CHAPTER THIRTEEN

The Prayer Life

All of the principles taught in this book are predicated on the prayer life. If after reading this book you don't spend more time in prayer, then you have just wasted your time reading this far. The development of your own personal prayer life, will become the strength of your marriage. God has shown me time and time again how important consistency is. The strength of your prayer life will come from its consistency. You may find yourself involved, at times, in a beautiful time of prayer that even goes for a number of hours. However, that will not accomplish as much as consistency will. God is not wanting us to approach praying simply as something we learn to master so we can get God to do things. Prayer is to become a lifestyle. The greatest changes I have found in my life through prayer have come because every day I give a minimum of an hour a day to God. The first thing we need to understand is the prayer habit.

Prayer Habit

The word "habit" is defined as something you have repeated so often that it becomes involuntary. Often we struggle with the word "habit" because of the connotations connected with that word. However, a habit is not inherently evil. You can have a good habit. Prayer would be classified as a good habit. Generally when I ask people if the prayer habit is easy to fall out of they respond by saying, "Yes." I disagree with that. You don't fall out of the habit of prayer any quicker than you fall out of any other habit. Wouldn't it be nice to just fall out of our bad habits? Suppose you had a terrible habit you wanted to get rid of but just couldn't, then one morning you got out of bed and fell right out of that bad habit which plagued you for many years. That would be classified as deliverance. You see there are really only two ways to get out of a habit. One is for God to deliver you. The other is for you to work your way out of it the same way you worked yourself into it. That being the case you can rest assured of one thing and that's that God is not going to deliver you from the habit of prayer. I've never encountered anyone who ever said, "I had this great habit of prayer but God delivered me from it." Therefore the only other way would be to work at not praying until you have quenched the spirit. So you see you don't just fall out of the prayer habit. Those who feel they fell right out of it probably never really fell into it.

The other problem we have with the word "habit" is all the legalism connected to the word. We don't want to get into bondage to prayer and find ourselves praying out of duty rather than desire. Therefore the motive behind your prayer life becomes all important. Legalism is basically trying to find favor with God through our actions. A legalistic approach to prayer would be that of praying to keep God pleased. Through that it would be easy to get into bondage to it. We should pray for one basic reason. We need to be in His presence. We need God. Even though the title of this book talks of prayer I am not trying to promote prayer. I am trying to promote God. God can change your marriage. However the most effective way to God is through the medium of prayer. However if all you want is a happy home, you could very well develop wrong motives for prayer. You must want God. Consider this, just think of how little you pray right now. Even in the midst of trouble it takes a lot to get us to pray. Suppose I introduced some principles of prayer that could instantly change your marriage. Most people would take those principles, apply them to their life, change their marriage, and then never spend any time with God after that. The only thing that will keep you seeking God, even after God answers your prayers, is for you to build a desire for God, not prayer. A pursuit of God continues even in the good times.

If you pray because you want God, then you recognize the need to make yourself pray because of what you lose if you don't. I make myself pray every day, not because I'm fearful that God will zap me if I don't, but rather, because of what I will gain in my relationship with God. Even though I make myself pray daily there is not one ounce of legalism in it.

The Habit Developed

Many individuals have a desire to pray, but can't put any feet to what they want, and subsequently feel defeated before they even start. There are three things I have found that will help considerably in the starting of a prayer life.

The first thing is a time goal. In Matthew 26:40 Jesus asks, "So, you men could not keep watch with Me for one hour?" In all of the Word of God the hour is the only reference to time and prayer. There is the exception of praying all night long, however, God is not expecting anyone to pray all night long every night. Every person should determine to spend a minimum of one hour a day in prayer.

A time goal is referring to the minimum amount of time you pray on a given day, never the maximum amount of time. We are not to tell God how much time we will pray. The time goal is to tell yourself how little time you will spend in prayer. This is a goal for you in the development of the prayer habit. It is not meant to regiment you, it is meant to give you some direction. For instance if you say, "Lord I'm going to pray at least an hour before I quit," then you find yourself getting so involved in your prayer time that you accidentally pray for two hours, God is not going to hold that against you. God is not going to say, "Maybe you'd better not pray tomorrow, you really over-did it today."

Exceeding your goal is not a problem. Making the goal is the problem, so you establish it for yourself. Keep in mind we are talking about what you must do to establish the habit of prayer. Some of those steps may seem very deliberate. The person with a well developed habit may not go through this at all, but he doesn't have to because prayer has its grips on him already.

Without a goal we don't push ourselves. The time goal helps make us pray. One of the reasons we stop short of praying as much as we want to is the fact that we have no goal in it. You see it's not unspiritual to make yourself pray. If after ten minutes of praying you feel like you're tired of prayer but yet you wanted to pray at least a half an hour, then you will make yourself continue to pray. If you had no goal you would just consider yourself done. To make yourself pray is no more unspiritual than making yourself read the Bible. Many times, in order to read the Bible through in a year, we will follow a prescribed plan and make ourselves read daily. Making yourself pray is no more unspiritual. Do you know what being unspiritual is? It's not praying when we know we should. If the Holy Spirit prompts us to prayer and we refuse, that's unspiritual; making yourself pray is not.

The second item in the development of the prayer life is that of having a set time to pray. By that I don't mean we have to pray at exactly the same time every day. It's just that every day you should determine when you will pray. In Acts 3:1 we read, "Now Peter and John were going up to the temple at the ninth hour, the hour of prayer." The hour of prayer in the New Testament was 3:00 pm. You may not be able to stick to a strict schedule, but you should establish daily a time for prayer. If you don't determine when you are going to pray you will find it to be one of the easiest things to put off.

Every day I look at my schedule and determine when I will have time in that particular day to spend time in prayer; I'm talking about my main time of prayer. This is not referring to the whole of my prayer life, this is only a reference to my primary prayer time. Some have said to me, "Isn't it unspiritual to determine when you are going to pray? Shouldn't you be led by the Spirit in this?" Certainly we should be led by God's Spirit in all things however, it is spiritual to make yourself pray also.

Obedience to God is also spiritual. In Luke 18:1 it states, "Now He was telling them a parable to show that at all times they ought to pray and not to lose heart." The word "ought" means an act of your will. Jesus is saying that the reason for this parable is to show that men by an act of their will must pray. If it is an act of their will, it means they weren't necessarily feeling the Spirit prompt them, they were simply praying out of obedience to God. If I determine that I have time to pray at 3:00 pm on a given day, that is not a problem. If I say, "God, I will pray at 3:00 pm today," why would that upset God? God will probably say, "It will be good to hear from you finally." If however I determine to pray at 3:00 pm, and at 1:00 pm I feel the Spirit tugging at my heart to go to prayer, I can. Just because I have established a set time for prayer does not mean I cannot pray at any other time. I can pray whenever God wants me to. It's just that if I am trying to establish the prayer habit in my life, then I need to determine when I will pray or chances are I will skip it. To pray when the Spirit prompts you is spiritual, however to pray out of obedience to God is just as spiritual.

Praying Without Ceasing

In the development of your prayer life, you need to establish a definite prayer time every day. However, that time of prayer is to develop into a life of prayer. Certainly there is a difference between a time of prayer and praying without ceasing. First Thessalonians 5:17 admonishes us to, "pray without ceasing." Praying without ceasing is that of developing such a God-consciousness about you that you go about your day in almost continual conversation with God. When you get into your car, you turn your thoughts to God and say, "Where were we, God? Oh yes, we were talking about that." It's praying at work, it's praying while you clean your house. Though our lives should continually be developing into a constant conversation with God, praying while you are doing other things should not constitute the whole of your prayer life.

We need, if for no other reason to set aside a definite time of prayer, to show God how important He is to us. It's no different than any other relationship. If I try to build a relationship with people by squeezing them into my schedule, I ultimately will make them feel that they are not important to me. For instance, if you invite me over to your home and say, "I want to talk to you about something important so please come over," so I come over and when I get there you say, "Come into the kitchen and we'll talk while I'm doing dishes." We try to carry on our conversation while you are doing the dishes. Then when you finish with that you say, "Now come into the living room and we can talk while I dust the furniture and vacuum the rug." So we are talking while you do that. Then you say, "Now that I'm finished with that come outside with me and we will talk while I mow the lawn and then shingle the roof." Pretty soon I would get the idea that I'm not important enough to you for you to set everything aside and spend time with me. Quite often that's what we want to do with God in our prayer life.

I will often encounter people who have an attitude toward prayer that simply justifies their lack of prayer. They say things like, "I'm building a relationship with God, prayer should be spontaneous, it shouldn't be scheduled." Or, "I don't believe in setting aside time just for prayer, I don't believe God wants me to do that. I believe that God simply wants me to stay in an attitude of prayer." I find that type of statement very interesting. If any person in all of human history was in a constant attitude of prayer it would have been Jesus. Yet Jesus found it necessary and essential that He get away for times of prayer. Even after a day of ministry, He would go up in the mountain and pray. Rising early in the morning, He would go out to pray. As Owen Carr once said,

"If Jesus needed to spend definite times in long private prayer, I need it even more." Pray without ceasing, but also set aside a definite time for prayer daily.

The third issue is that of priority. Prayer must be a priority. In Matthew 21:13 Jesus said, "My house shall be called a house of prayer." In that statement Jesus makes prayer pre-eminent. Jesus says prayer should stand over and above everything else. If prayer is not a priority you will never develop a life of prayer. At our morning prayer meeting at our church in Kenosha, Wisconsin, we were at the church every morning at 6:30 a.m. Shortly after we started, some of our associate pastors noted to me that in order to maintain this new lifestyle they were starting to watch the 9:00 p.m. news rather than the 10:00 p.m. news. What they were saying is that they were adjusting their lifestyle in order to pray each morning.

One of our problems is our approach to prayer. We are saying, "Here is my lifestyle, there is no room for prayer." Instead we must say, "Here is prayer, how must my lifestyle change in order to work it into my life?" We must treat prayer with the same principles we treat money. We teach tithing and principles of giving, not on the basis of what we can afford to give, but rather on the basis that we can't afford not to give; that, in fact, if we will honor God with our tithe, God will honor us with more money. We seem to understand this principle when it comes to giving, but haven't transferred that same principle over to time yet. The same principle stands true that if you will honor God with your time, God will give you more time.

If you say, "I don't tithe because I can't afford to tithe," then you will never be able to afford to tithe. You tithe so you can afford to tithe. It's a step of faith. The same is true with time and prayer. If you are saying that the reason you don't pray is because you have no time, then you will never have time to pray. You must honor God with your time in prayer, and then God will give you more time to pray. The only time you have time to pray is when you start making time for prayer. God will give you more time. I don't know how God does it any more than I know how God increases your income through tithing. We just take it by faith.

I began my prayer life when I was a student in seminary. I was working in a restaurant from midnight until 6:00 am. Then at 7:00 am I would drive the forty-five minute commute to seminary and be in classes until 1:00 pm. Then I would drive home and be there around 2:00 pm. I then had around ten hours to get some sleep, do all my studies, and try to maintain some type of communication with my wife. At midnight it was back to work. In the midst of that, I decided to give God a minimum of an hour a day in prayer. Within a short time, I expanded it to an hour and a half and then two hours a day. I have no idea where the time came from but as I honored God with my time He gave me more.

If you do not have a priority of prayer, you will encounter all kinds of interruptions the moment you decide to pray. When a person decides to pray, the phone rings off the wall, the children demand all of your attention, and of course your mind starts thinking of everything else you have to do. If that is the case, it could be that you are choosing the wrong time of the day for prayer. There is a time when the children are quiet and the phone is not ringing. However, it takes a priority of prayer to pull yourself out of bed early in the morning just to spend time with God.

There is a simple fact of life that we all live by; we do what is important to us. There is no way to get around that. The things we place a priority on are the things we are giving ourselves to. When our pursuit of God takes preeminence, then we will pray regardless of the price we have to pay. It all boils down to this one question: Do we want God?

One of the most prayerful churches I have been in is Rev. Jim Thompson's church in Lodi, Wisconsin. Rev. Thompson promotes the hour of prayer, and it shows in his congregation. I had just finished teaching on prayer one evening when I was sitting in the pew with the father of three young children. One of his children (three years old) would go up to his mom, who was praying at the altar, and get as close to her as he could without touching her. I asked the father what the child was doing. He said, "Their mom has taught all of our children that when she is praying they are not allowed to touch or interrupt her." That mom is teaching her children that the most important thing in her life is her pursuit of God. Believe me, God will honor that; her children will grow up with a deep sense of the fear of God in their lives.

CHAPTER FOURTEEN

The Hour Of Prayer

"Lord, teach us to pray just as John also taught his disciples."
—*Disciples of Jesus*

Because my ministry deals exclusively with prayer, after I preach, I am usually approached by people with questions about prayer. Very few people ask me if I think that they should pray. Most believers I talk to after services want to develop a prayer habit, but they simply don't know where to begin—or perhaps when to begin. Time seems to be a perplexing matter for many, and it is the basis for the most frequently asked questions. How do you spend quality time in prayer without repeating yourself? How do you keep your thoughts from wandering? Those and many other questions about prayer seem to plague us today. In this chapter we will look at the hour of prayer itself.

First of all it is important to have some type of design or structure to your prayer time. This is especially true for the beginner, the person trying to develop his prayer life. Structure keeps us on the right track and helps us become intense in what we are doing, especially when it comes to prayer. If we don't have any kind of design to follow, we'll end up waiting for a certain mood to strike us and then lead us. When that mood doesn't strike us, we have nothing to follow and our mind begins to wander. Wandering thoughts almost always come from the lack of structure. If you don't know where you're headed in advance, you won't be able to give yourself to prayer in the manner you should.

In my growing up years my family was very involved in automobiles and various types of automobile racing. If we were going to be involved in a race where the course had a lot of turns and twists to it, it was a good practice to go over the course a few times before the race began. If you are going down the straightaway and you don't know which way you'll have to turn, you'll have to slow down because you won't be able to take the curve at your maximum intensity. If, however, you know the course well and you're certain where each twist and turn is, you can maintain maximum intensity.

In prayer we need a plan. We need to know the course we are on. If we have a foreknowledge of all the areas we will cover in our prayer time, then we can give ourself entirely to the area we are on. For instance, if your time of prayer begins with worship, and yet you have the foreknowledge that you will eventually pray for others (intercession), then during worship you concentrate on nothing else. You won't have to be worrying that you may forget to pray for others. You can give yourself entirely to worshiping God without being distracted by mental notes reminding you to do this or that. If you don't have a plan, you will most likely go into your prayer time floundering until you think of something to pray for. You will pray for that until another thought comes to mind, at which time you will start praying about that. Then suddenly an even more important thought may occur to you. Pretty soon your mind is going from one thought to another and before you know it you are daydreaming. If you do that enough, you will get so discouraged with prayer that you will say, "What's the use?"

I want to introduce to you a very simple way to begin praying an hour a day. For our design we will use the Lord's Prayer found in Matthew 6:9-13. Many individuals have used this prayer as a basis for spending time with God. Some go into great detail, others do not. I don't. Keep in mind I am not trying to lay out a prayer for you to pray. These will be guidelines at best. The praying is up to you. The Lord's Prayer breaks down into five major areas.

1. **Worship**. "Our Father who art in heaven, Hallowed be Thy name" (Matt. 6:9). Jesus begins this prayer by bringing praise and worship to the name of His Father. Your time of prayer should begin with worship. We need to begin by focusing all of our attention on our God. We need to centralize God and decentralize self. Simply tell Him how much you love Him, and how much you need Him. Concentrate on who He is. Do a study on the names of God (i.e., Jehovah Jireh ["God is our provider"]).

Worship is the primary element of your prayer time, which develops intimacy between you and God. The whole purpose of prayer is to get to know our God. Worship opens up those avenues of intimacy. Spend a minimum of ten minutes worshiping God.

2. **Intercession**. "Thy kingdom come. Thy will be done" (Matt. 6:10). Intercession is simply praying for others. Praying for the kingdom of God is praying for souls to come to know Christ. It's also praying for those who are already a part of that Kingdom. This is the area where you should pray for your family first, then friends, and then the world. Intercession should comprise the single largest portion of your prayer time. You should plan to spend at least thirty minutes in intercession. Thirty minutes may seem like a lot of time until you break it down into six, five-minute sessions. If you can think of six people to pray for, you will find this half hour going by much faster than you ever thought possible. Most people need more than just five minutes of prayer. The point I'm making here is that it really isn't difficult to spend time in prayer when you have a plan. What you will most likely find is that thirty minutes is not enough time to pray for your family, friends, and the world.

3. **Petition.** "Give us this day our daily bread" (Matt. 6:11). Petition is praying for yourself. This is the area where you bring your needs before God. "Give us this day," can literally mean our sustenance, or physical needs. However we have spiritual needs that should not be overlooked. Don't be afraid to pray for your needs. God wants to meet your needs more than you realize. You should spend a minimum of five minutes in this area.

4. **Confession.** "And forgive us our debts, as we also have forgiven our debtors" (Matt. 6:12). "Forgive us,"—those words are some of the most important words we will ever say. They need to be included in your prayer time daily. Every day we need to ask God to search our hearts. I was once counseling with a lady who made an interesting comment to me about her own relationship with God. She said, "I keep a short account with God." She meant that whenever she does something she considers sinful she quickly asks God to forgive her. If you will daily ask God to search your heart He can keep you from the kind of involvement with sin that ruins lives. You should spend a minimum of five minutes in confession.

5. **Praise.** "...For Thine is the kingdom, and the power, and the glory, forever. Amen" (Matt. 6:13). Jesus begins this prayer worshiping God, and He ends it by praising God. This is simply a repeat of the first step. You should spend a minimum of ten minutes in this step.

The Lord's Prayer is designed to develop balance in your prayer life. All of the essential areas of prayer are covered in it. If you will notice how the time breaks down, you will see that you are spending a total of twenty minutes focusing strictly on God through worship (steps 1 and 5). You are spending thirty minutes focusing in on others (step 2). Plus you are spending ten minutes focusing in on yourself (steps 3 and 4). That totals sixty minutes. It is a very simple, structured approach to prayer. (See figure 1A p. 137.)

Break Down of the Hour of Prayer

Based on the Lord's Prayer (Matt. 6:9-13)

Figure 1A

1. **Worship**; Matthew 6:9; "Our Father who art in heaven, Hallowed be Thy name."
Spend a minimum of ten minutes worshiping God.

2. **Intercession**; Matthew 6:10; "Thy kingdom come. Thy will be done."
Spend a minimum of thirty minutes praying for others.

3. **Petition**; Matthew 6:11; "Give us this day our daily bread."
Spend a minimum of five minutes praying for your needs.

4. **Confession**; Matthew 6:12; "And forgive us our debts, as we also have forgiven our debtors."
Spend a minimum of five minutes asking God to search your heart so that you may confess any sin.

5. **Praise**; Matthew 6:13; "...For Thine is the kingdom, and the power, and the glory, forever. Amen."
Spend a minimum of ten minutes praising God.

CHAPTER FIFTEEN

Praying For The Rebellious

If Christians spent as much time praying as they do grumbling, they would soon have nothing to grumble about.
—Anonymous

One of the purposes of this book is to give hope to the individual that feels there is no hope. If you fit into this category, rest assured that you have great reason for hope. If your spouse or your children are not saved, you have cause to look to the future with great anticipation. God has provided principles for you to follow which will make you a co-laborer with Him, working together to bring your loved ones to salvation.

For though we walk in the flesh, we do not war according to the flesh, for the weapons of our warfare are not of the flesh, but divinely powerful for the destruction of fortresses. We are destroying speculations and every lofty thing raised up against the knowledge of God, and we are taking every thought captive to the obedience of Christ,

and we are ready to punish all disobedience, whenever
your obedience is complete (2 Cor. 10:3-6).

Right now we are encased in a body made of flesh and
blood. However, the war in which we fight is a spiritual one,
against non-corporeal entities—beings who do not have bodies
in the sense we are accustomed to thinking. They have a
profound influence on the unsaved who are already enslaved
to their sinful natures. These demonic forces and man's own
fallen sinful nature exist on an invisible spiritual plain and
their effects can be seen in our visible world. But we must
clearly understand that they are of a spiritual nature and
cannot be engaged by physical means. God has provided us
with spiritual armaments to fight with. They are not carnal,
but are divinely powerful; that is, only powerful through
God. However, we are no longer engaged in a spiritual battle
if we try to force change by physical persuasion or physical
coercion, relying on our own ingenuity or abilities. If we
forsake God's methods in favor of ours, we will be quite on
our own. We cannot expect God's assistance if we will not do
things God's way. If however we choose to do things according to Scripture, we can expect great things to happen.

First of all, as in any battle, you must define your
objective. Verse five gives us just that. After defining the
battle, it concludes by telling us that there are certain things
in the life of the individual you are praying for that keep them
from knowing God. Your objective then is to pray that the one
you are praying for will come to a knowledge of God. The
whole purpose of your praying for them should be that they
would get to know God in an intimate way.

Your objective must be pure in order to expect God to
help you. We are not to pray some type of vengeance on them
as Jesus' disciples wanted to do when they asked Him if they
should call down fire on the Samaritans. If you start praying,
"God, get them back for all the years they got me," you can
rest assured that you are on your own. God is no more
interested in giving them what they deserve than He was in
giving you what you deserve. We are all recipients of grace

and had better thank God that He didn't exercise vengeance on us. When you pray, you ought to address the problem at hand.

The whole problem with unbelievers is that they simply have no intimacy with God; they don't know God. They spend very little time (if any) with God. This is a spiritual problem, and the only way to address a spiritual problem is through spiritual means, namely prayer. We must engage in this battle through prayer. There just isn't any other way. Through prayer we may be prompted to take certain physical action, but that is not always the case and is, in any event, completely up to God. Our primary concern is prayer, and in 2 Corinthians 10:3-6, God has listed three things that are raised up in an individual's life that keep him from knowing God.

Strongholds

First we are to destroy fortresses. The King James Version reads, "pulling down of strongholds." In the Greek language the word we translate "stronghold" means "fortress" or "prison." In either case, it is something that is characterized by impregnable walls. In the spiritual world, these walls keep people from God. They cannot see beyond those walls. They sense they are cut off from God, but they feel they cannot get to know God because of the walls. Our objective then is to destroy or pull down these walls. In order to do that, we need to determine what the walls are made of.

A stronghold can be something that is very deep-seated. It may be something that goes back to childhood. It can be constructed out of habits, complexes, or deeply-rooted problems that literally imprison them. Keep in mind we are talking about people who either have never made a commitment to Christ or who have given up on their faith.

The stronghold may not be as simple to determine as you think. It's not always the obvious when dealing with spiritual matters. You may say, "I know their stronghold. It's alcohol." Alcohol may not necessarily be a person's stronghold. Alcohol may simply be how the stronghold manifests itself. What we need to deal with is the root cause of that alcoholism. Why does this person drink? Only God knows.

The first step in our warfare prayer is to ask God to reveal the individual's stronghold to you. Ask God to show you what has that person in prison. This may take some time. You may not find it right away. Simply make it a matter of prayer every day until you feel God has shown you what you need to know. Remember it's a battle. Therefore you may encounter some spiritual opposition. You could possibly run into the kind of opposition Daniel did in Chapter 10 of his book. Daniel prayed for twenty-one days straight before God's messenger could bring the message to him. God's forces encountered a battle in bringing the answer. Satan has the person you are praying for in his grips. He is not about to give up without a fight.

Speculations

Secondly we are to destroy speculations. The King James Version calls it, "casting down imaginations." In Greek the word "speculations" or "imaginations" has several different meanings. One of the Greek meanings is, "the designs of the heathen," meaning "the thought processes of the heathen." In other words, it's the thought processes of men who do not know the power of God. If you do not understand the power of God, you have very little hope. What happens is this: after being in a prison (stronghold) long enough, and not knowing the power of God, you begin to tell yourself things that are not true. You begin to say to yourself, "I have tried everything and nothing will help me." Those thoughts (speculations) are what keep a person in his prison.

Another meaning for the word "speculation" is "an argument which is correct as far as things appear, but which is actually invalid." What they are telling themselves based on what they see seems to be correct, but it is actually an invalid argument because with God it doesn't matter how things appear. With God all things are possible. So no matter how things look on the surface, God can make them different. However the person who is living in these imaginations cannot see that God can make a difference. This is where the battle continues. This is where we need to ask God to open their spiritual eyes.

The second step in our warfare prayer is to ask God to renew their minds. In Romans 12:2 it says, "...but be transformed by the renewing of your mind...." As our minds are renewed, we are transformed. We are seeking to transform the individuals we are praying for. They are in a mental prison, and we can set them free through prayer as we petition God to renew their minds. Ask God to enlighten them spiritually. Pray a protective hedge around their minds. Pray that all wrong influences would leave their lives. As God begins to renew their minds, they will begin to think as God thinks and not as man thinks.

Pride

The third area of prayer is that of "lofty things." The King James Version calls it, "high things." Both mean pride. Pride is one of the greatest struggles any person has in their relationship with God. Even if you are successful in pulling down their stronghold and casting down their imaginations you may still have an uphill battle on your hands.

The only breaking of pride we find in the Scriptures comes through a revelation of Christ. Saul was a very proud man, a Hebrew of the Hebrews, of the tribe of Benjamin and highly educated. Then in a moment's time, as he saw Jesus, his life was drastically changed. He was no longer the proud Pharisee, but rather a humble man subject to what God wanted for him.

So how is the person you are praying for going to see Jesus? Going back to our text in verse six we read, "and we are ready to punish all disobedience, whenever your obedience is complete." Our own obedience will make our prayers for the disobedience of someone else effective. If I understand that my prayer for my family's obedience to God will be more effective through my own obedience to God, I should try to be more obedient. Our becoming obedient to God is the process of developing in the character of Christ. Through our obedience to God, others will see Jesus in us. In other words, the one you are praying for will see Jesus in you. You are the revelation of Christ that will ultimately humble them.

Redirecting the Rebellious Heart

What can a parent do to gain the respect of a rebellious teenager? Given the fact that they are teenagers, you are faced with a problem that must be handled differently than if they were still preteen. I talked once with a lady whose thirteen-year-old girl treated her with great disrespect. She said if she ever did try to take a strong stand, her daughter would grab her (mom) by the arm and threaten her. Our first reaction to that is to say, "That cannot be, you cannot allow your daughter to do that."

When it comes to developing respect in a child, it is best to do it at a very young age. When a child is young you can demand certain behavior from them. If they will not respond, you know you can spank them without them retaliating. The purpose for demanding respect is because the respect they develop for the parent is eventually transferred to God. If a young child learns to respect his elders, and especially parents, he ultimately learns to respect his God.

In our society today, everything is upside down. Many children live in less than desirable situations. Many of them live in broken homes. Many of them live with other children that are not their own flesh and blood siblings. Many of them are tossed back and forth by parents that really don't want the responsibility of raising them. In light of all this, many children have never been taught the respect they should have for their parents. By the time they become teenagers, it becomes obvious that there are great problems between parent and child.

Trying to demand respect will never work in a society that really doesn't care for its children. If a young child learns to respect his parents, that respect will transfer to God. However if a teenager has no respect for his parents he will rarely have any respect for God either. At this point we must realize we are dealing with a spiritual issue. You are dealing with a rebellious, proud spirit. The only way to counter a proud spirit is through a humble spirit.

If an Old Testament prophet would come into a town to preach repentance and found he could not gain the people's respect, he would go to the town square and begin to weep. After some time, the people of the town would begin to realize their own sinfulness and repent. The prophet's humble spirit would finally break the proud, rebellious spirit of the town. When it comes to a spiritual battle, we cannot counter a satanic spirit by using a satanic spirit. Pride is satanic. Rebellion is satanic. If you are dealing with a rebellious teenager, the only thing that will break it in his own life is your humble spirit.

You need to sit down with your rebellious child some day and begin to talk about what they are doing wrong. Prior to doing that ask God to express His broken heart through you. Ask God to show your teen how their sin is breaking the heart of God. Literally, bring yourself to a place of tears just as the Old Testament prophets had to do and weep before your child.

The key here is that of expressing God's heart not yours. Don't tell them how much they are hurting you, remember they have no respect for you and are not impressed with whether they are hurting you or not. Since they have lost respect for you, the only thing you can do is to cause them to respect God. Once they gain a new respect for God, that will be transferred back to you. If they begin to believe that God actually cares for them, they will begin to respect God. However, they will never see God through you taking a firm stand against them. That which will destroy their proud, rebellious heart will be your humble, submissive heart for God.

As one of the characters in the comic strip "Pogo" observed many years ago, "We have seen the enemy, and he is us." We are often the greatest hindrance to prayer we face. We determine how quickly God will work in others by how quickly we allow God to change us. God wants to change the person you are praying for, but He wants to change them by causing them to see Christ in you. The pray-er holds the key to change. His own submission to God brings others into submission.

Even though the thrust of this book is to help your home, it is not a book that just gives you formulas. I reiterate, prayer is to become a lifestyle. Just because you have struggles at home does not mean you must spend all your time praying for your family. It's not praying for them that will change them, it's the development of your prayer life that will change them. God changes others through the changes prayer brings into the pray-er. Even if you are praying for Africa, your family will be effected because when you are praying—even for Africa—you, too, are effected. No matter what you are praying for when you pray, you are spending time in God's presence. It's God's presence that changes people, not just prayer.

CHAPTER SIXTEEN

Praying For Your Family

A happy family is but an earlier heaven.
—Sir John Bowring

Nothing is more dear to the heart of the caring parent than the spiritual condition of his or her family. A great spiritual gulf separates a believer from a non-believing family member. The sense of intimacy and family is lost. Praying for your family then becomes a primary concern since there is no other single, more important thing a parent can do for the family.

And Jesus kept increasing in wisdom and stature, and in favor with God and men (Luke 2:52).

We find that there were four basic areas of growth in Jesus' life. They are the same areas all of us strive to grow in. If you pray for your family members to grow in these areas, you will be praying a very complete prayer for them.

Wisdom

The Bible tells us that as Jesus grew, He increased in

wisdom. As parents, we make certain mental demands on our children. We want them to get good grades. However, when they don't do something correctly, the only help we often give them is to tell them, "Think!" If we are making these demands, we should also be praying for them that they would grow in the same area.

When my wife, Lou Ann, became pregnant I began to pray for our unborn baby. I might add that because it was not yet born, I didn't know if it was going to be a boy or a girl, therefore I didn't know whether I was going to be a father or a mother (obviously nobody prayed that I'd grow in wisdom). During this period of time, I was teaching a prayer seminar in Maple Grove, Minnesota. One evening I had gone to the church to pray before the service. I had been praying for several weeks for our child to grow in the four areas of growth found in Luke 2:52. When I came to the area of wisdom, God impressed upon my heart to pray that this child would fear Him. To fear God is to respect God or reverence God. This is why the Bible says, "The fear of the Lord is the beginning of wisdom." There is no wiser thing a person can do than to respect His God. Since that night I rarely pray for my son without praying that he would have a deep sense of the fear of God in his life.

I have found Isaiah 11:2,3 to be an excellent portion of Scripture to use in praying for one's children. It covers many of the areas of growth we are concerned with. In praying the Scriptures, insert your child's name wherever it is appropriate. As an example, I will show you what that prayer is like: "Father, I pray that the Spirit of the Lord will rest upon (name), the spirit of wisdom and understanding, the spirit of counsel and strength, the spirit of knowledge and the fear of the Lord. Make (name) of quick understanding in the fear of the Lord; and help (name) not to judge after the sight of his eyes, neither judge after the hearing of his ears." That prayer covers the next area of growth that we are concerned with also, the social area.

Social

Jesus increased in favor with man. In the previous prayer (Isaiah 11), you are praying that they would not make judgments about others by what they see nor that they would reprove others simply by what they hear. You are actually praying for them to treat others fairly, which will obviously help them in the area of social growth. Another important area you have just prayed for is the spirit of counsel and might to be upon them. This is quite significant because you are actually praying for them to be leaders of others rather than followers. To pray for their social growth also addresses the issue of peer pressure. We all want our children to choose the right kind of friends. Praying for their social growth gives God a greater opportunity to influence them in those critical decisions.

Health

Jesus increased in stature. This is probably one of the most prayed for areas there is. How many times have pregnant ladies been asked if it was a boy or a girl and their response was, "It doesn't matter as long as it's healthy,"? Our children's physical development is very important to us and to God.

Spiritual Growth

Jesus also increased in favor with God. What could be more important than this? This certainly tops the priority list, but it should not be the only thing we pray for. The first pastor I ever worked for told me he always prayed that his children would maintain a tender heart toward God. Obviously we want our children to grow spiritually. We want them to find favor with God. Along with spiritual growth, we must add all the other areas of growth. We don't want children that are so heavenly minded they are of no earthly good. Neither do we want children that are so earthly minded they are no heavenly good. In all of this we want balance in their lives.

Diligence

God will do many great things for your family as you pray for them. I remember James Dobson telling of his grandfather who, at one time in his life, decided to pray one hour a day for his family. To this day all of his grandchildren are serving the Lord.

> *Only take heed to yourself and keep your soul diligently,*
> *lest you forget the things which your eyes have seen, and*
> *lest they depart from your heart all the days of your life;*
> *but make them known to your sons and your grandsons*
> *(Deut. 4:9).*

When it comes to praying for our children, we, as parents, must maintain a diligent relationship with God. We need to remember the things we have seen God do so we can pass them on to our children and our grandchildren. I was doing a seminar near Canada once when I went to the church early to pray. After I was there for some time, the janitor of the church came and we started talking. He was an elderly man who had attended the church for many years. Not long after we had started talking, I came to realize that this man was a man full of bitterness and anger. Instead of sharing his wisdom with me, he had nothing at all to tell me about God. I was expecting this man's collected years and acquired wisdom to teach me some things about God; instead, all I got was backbiting and gossip. As I sat there I thought, "What a shame, here is a man, a father of Israel, and he has nothing to offer me." This is why the verse said that we should keep our souls diligently. I fully intend, should the Lord tarry, to sit with my son and teach him the things God has taught me. The younger generation needs the wisdom of gray hair.

One time a pastor who was hurting approached my mom and dad. He was in the midst of some struggles in his church and with a trembling voice he said, "Would you two come and give me some counsel, I need the gray hair." I have a concern that the old guard has dropped her guard today. Instead of being a bastion of righteousness and strong standards, I am finding that many have critical, unkind spirits. The "gray hairs" in the church should be the most powerful group in the church. They are the ones with time to seek God. They are the ones that remember how things used to be. If they do not hold that strong standard and teach the upcoming generation how to seek God, we will continue to loose our heritage.

In *Refiners Fire, Volume 1*, P.T. Forsythe says, "Prayer is one form of sacrifice, but if it is the only form, it is vain oblation." If we are praying for our children, that's good, but it cannot be the only thing we are doing for our children.

Prayer is in itself a sacrifice, but it cannot be the only sacrifice I make. I know many parents that are praying for their children's salvation and yet they do nothing to live a consecrated life before them. Forsythe goes on to say, "If we pray for our children that they may have God's blessing, we are really promising that nothing shall be lacking on our part to be a divine blessing to them. If we have no kind of religious relation to them, our prayer is quite unreal and its failure should not be a surprise."

If we are asking God to bless our children, we are really telling God that we will do all we can to be a divine blessing to our children. We are telling God we will sincerely seek Him so that God can bless our children through who we are. We must remember what Forsythe said: that if we fail to seek God, our prayer is quite unreal and its failure should not surprise us. Prayer is to become a lifestyle, not just something you do to make sure God blesses your children. If I am praying and asking God to do something for someone else and yet remain disobedient to Him in other areas, that prayer is vain (empty) oblation.

CHAPTER SEVENTEEN

Praying As A Family

The family that prays together stays together.
—Author Unknown

Establishing family devotions is one of the most challenging tasks any family can face. Sometimes the enormous task is not even attempted because people figure that they have church services to attend together as much as three times per week. Also, it is often pointed out that the young people have their own special youth meetings to attend, the children likewise, and the parents have men's ministry groups and women's ministry groups. With all of this church activity, family devotions are considered unnecessary. In spite of these popular beliefs, I believe family devotions are important. I have no intentions detailing formats used to conduct family devotions. There are already many books written on that subject, and they can give you all the guidance you will ever need on how to have devotions. My objective is to convince you that you need to pick up one of those books or begin your own strategy for family devotions.

When I read in Hebrews 10:25 that we are not to forsake the assembling of ourselves together, I don't just think of the importance of attending church services. I also think about how important it is for the family to meet together spiritually. The family is a mini church. The husband acts as Christ, the wife as pastor, and the children as the congregation. This role of the wife explains why she is often the one instilling values in the children. She generally spends more time with the children than her husband does. This is not to say that the husband's role is unimportant. Indeed, his role in the family is as important as Christ's role in the Church.

The Basics of Family Devotions: Prayer and the Bible

> *...From childhood you have known the sacred writings which are able to give you the wisdom that leads to salvation through faith which is in Christ Jesus (2 Tim. 3:15).*

In this letter to his long-time friend and disciple, Paul, writing shortly before his death, reflected on the importance of Timothy's knowledge of Scripture since childhood. Timothy had a godly mother and a godly grandmother who apparently read God's Word to him as a small child. This demonstrates the importance of family devotions, regardless of a child's age. It also highlights one of the two basic areas every family devotions should include: the Bible. It's difficult to argue the validity of reading the Bible to young children with results like these; Timothy turned out okay.

> *And it came about that while He was praying in a certain place, after He had finished, one of His disciples said to Him, "Lord, teach us to pray just as John also taught his disciples" (Luke 11:1).*

Along with God's Word, we need prayer. It's valuable for children to see their parents praying, far more valuable than only hearing their parents tell them they should pray. In addition, it is instructional. They learn far more from the example of seeing their parents praying consistently than from any Sunday school teaching about the importance of prayer.

Results Take Time

Family devotions don't always accomplish immediate results. However, the one thing I do see family devotions do, which makes them very important, is that they are instilling attitudes in your children. As stated earlier, the greatest benefit for children is in the long term as they see their parent's example. Through family devotions, you are telling your children that prayer and God's Word are important to you as parents.

One of the greatest frustrations of family devotions is that many parents spend more time telling their children to be still and listen than they do anything else. It is very easy to start thinking that there is not much benefit in doing devotions at this point in life and that maybe they would get more out of it when they are older. That would be like deciding not to take your children to church because they're too young to get anything out of it, and they prevent you from getting as much out of it as you would like with their continual distractions. Believe it or not, their church attendance or presence at family devotions is not the most important thing taking place. The primary goal of all spiritual activity is to develop attitudes in your children. Even if you feel your children are not getting much out of devotions, they are getting at least one thing: a favorable attitude toward prayer and God's Word.

Psychologists tell us that once a child reaches the age of twenty, give or take a couple years, they generally revert back to their parents' values. They may go through their years of rebellion, but as they mature, they begin to do things the same way mom and dad used to. This is not without its exceptions, nor should it be. There are many cases in which a child surrenders his life to Christ, but his parents do not. In those cases, it is unlikely that the child will go back to his parents' values. I remember thinking as a teenager just how little my parents knew about anything. I was young and had all the answers to all the problems facing mankind. I was amazed at how smart my parents became by the time I was twenty. By that time, I decided to do things the way mom and dad did things. Though psychologists have only recently discovered this, the Bible has taught if for thousands of years.

> *Train up a child in the way he should go, even when he*
> *is old he will not depart from it (Prov. 22:6).*

I learned the truth of this while I was a youth pastor and while I was working on my Masters Degree, which specialized in youth ministries, and it has always remained true. When you are working with the early teens (twelve to sixteen), you can get them to do just about anything your youth group is going to do. However, by the time they reach the upper levels of high school, their involvement reflects their parents' commitment to God. If mom and dad stayed faithful in their pursuit of God and church attendance, then the kids were still workable. If, on the other hand, mom and dad had a lackadaisical attitude for those things, so did their children. As they get older, they do not depart from what they have been taught. Don't overly concern yourself with what you feel is presently being accomplished through your family devotions. Keep in mind that you are instilling attitudes in their lives that will one day begin to lead them.

CHAPTER EIGHTEEN

Praying Through

We must endure, or all is lost.
—Sir Winston Churchill

There are teachers and preachers today who contend that one who prays about a given matter more than once lacks faith. They teach that if you really have faith, God will answer your prayer and you won't need to pray a second time. My experience and my study of God's Word has taught me that this isn't always so. There are times when continuing to pray for something is because of faith, not because of a lack of faith. I once heard the Rev. James Singleton from Fort Worth preach about three distinct places where God's people were required to continue praying about something as an act of faith.

The First Example: Habakkuk

How long, O Lord, will I call for help, and Thou wilt not hear? I cry out to Thee, "Violence!" Yet Thou does not save (Hab. 1:2).

In this first instance, the prophet was praying about the devastation that was taking place in his country. God had given him a vision of the good he was going to do for His people, yet all Habakkuk could see was destruction and devastation. It seemed to him as if God was ignoring his cries. Yet Habakkuk resolved that he would do the only thing he could do: he would continue to pray.

> *I will stand on my guard post and station myself on the rampart; and I will keep watch to see what He will speak to me, and how I may reply when I am reproved (Hab. 2:1).*

The prophet kept his watch. He continued to pray and watched to see what God was going to say. Finally, God did indeed answer Habakkuk.

> *Then the Lord answered me and said, "Record the vision and inscribe it on tablets, that the one who reads it may run. For the vision is yet for the appointed time; it hastens toward the goal, and it will not fail. Though it tarries, wait for it; for it will certainly come, it will not delay (Hab. 2:2,3).*

God's answer to him was not what Habakkuk had anticipated. Although God answered him, He did not provide the explanation the prophet had hoped to hear, nor did He put an immediate end to the suffering of His people. He just told Habakkuk to continue praying. It wasn't the appointed time. The answer was on its way, but it wasn't there yet. Habakkuk just had to remain faithful in prayer and wait. He went on to tell His servant that the just will live by faith.

> *Behold, as for the proud one, His soul is not right within him; but the righteous will live by his faith (Hab. 2:4).*

God presented Habakkuk with a clear depiction of a person who lives by faith; he is a person who is completely dependent upon God. There is no pride in him. He realizes that God is all that he has and that without God he is nothing. It says that the just live by this kind of faith and continue to pray.

The Second Example: Jesus

Now He was telling them a parable to show that at all times they ought to pray and not lose heart, saying, "There was in a certain city a judge who did not fear God, and did not respect man. And there was a widow in that city, and she kept coming to him, saying, 'Give me legal protection from my opponent.' And for a while he was unwilling; but afterward he said to himself, 'Even though I do not fear God nor respect man, yet because this widow bothers me, I will give her legal protection, lest by continually coming she wear me out.'" And the Lord said, "Hear what the unrighteous judge said; now shall not God bring about justice for His elect, who cry out to Him day and night, and will He delay long over them? I tell you that He will bring about justice for them speedily. However, when the Son of Man comes, will He find faith on the earth?" (Luke 18:1-8).

There is little room for commentary here. Jesus was very clear. He said the whole purpose of this parable is to teach those that are praying not to quit praying. In fact, in verse eight, He implies that one's continued praying is a statement of faith, not a lack of faith.

In the last two cases, God has instructed His people to continue praying as an exercise of faith. Does this mean God delights in holding back answers to our prayers? Of course, God does not find any pleasure in holding back the answers to our prayers, but sometimes He has to. That's because today believers are focussing on the answers to their prayers more than they are focussing on God. When we concentrate on the answers to our prayers, we fail to see what God is doing through our prayers. Prayer is meant to change the pray-er as much as or more than the thing we are praying about. Since people don't understand that God is changing them through their praying, they fail to see a need to continue praying.

Patience Through Prayer

Consider it all joy, my brethren, when you encounter various trials, knowing that the testing of your faith produces endurance. And let endurance have its perfect result, that you may be perfect and complete, lacking in nothing. But if any of you lacks wisdom, let him ask of God, who gives to all men generously and without reproach, and it will be given to him. But let him ask in faith without any doubting, for the one who doubts is like the surf of the sea driven and tossed by the wind. For let not that man expect that he will receive anything from the Lord, being a double-minded man, unstable in all his ways (James 1:2-8).

James began his letter by telling his readers that trials are good for us because they produce patience (endurance), and we need patience. Then he went on to describe what patience is. He explained that it is exhibited when one asks of God in faith, without doubting. Patience also involved endurance, and James also described one who lacks endurance, likening him to a wave of the sea. That man is tossed about to and fro, carried about with every wind of doctrine. God doesn't want us to be like that. He wants to develop stability in us, the ability to endure. The only time He can develop those qualities in us is in prayer. Prayer is the only way.

There are many things that cannot be attained except through prayer; ministry, for instance. Pray-Tell Ministries is a consequence of my spending time with God. I didn't just sit down one day and say, "Today, I will create a ministry centered around prayer." None of us can go out and seek to create an effective ministry. We must seek to live a life pleasing to God. Out of the discipline that develops, God will say, "Because you allowed Me to teach you, I am going to use you to teach others."

Amazingly, it was my weaknesses that drove me to prayer. My weaknesses were driving me farther and farther from God. I never questioned my salvation, but a gap between God and me was widening, causing great depression. I knew the things I was doing didn't please God, and I wanted to please God. Finally, I began to invest hours in prayer, just telling God that I wanted Him and needed Him. One night in prayer, I said, "God, I've had enough. I'm tired of these weaknesses. I'm tired of struggling with them. I'm tired of how they hurt you. I'm even tired of being tired of them." I pleaded with God to miraculously remove those weaknesses from my life. But I sensed God's voice replying, "Ron, I can remove those weaknesses from your life, but if I do, you'll never become what you will if your pray them through." You see, God isn't as concerned about your weaknesses as He is about you drawing from His strength to overcome them. God showed me He was using my weaknesses to develop His strength in me by causing me to pray.

Drawing From God's Strength

Concerning this I entreated the Lord three times that it might depart from me. And He said to Me, "My grace is sufficient for you, for power is perfected in weakness..." (2 Cor. 12:8,9).

Paul had been asking God to remove a "thorn in his flesh." Theologians debate what that "thorn" was. Roman medical technology of Paul's day was actually advanced enough to permit some successful tracheotomies (though the lack of anesthetics proved to be a problem). It seems that a thorn in one's flesh would not overwhelm a physician of that time and place. Some theologians contend that it was not a literal thorn, but that the term was a figure of speech back then referring to some kind of other problem. In either case, it is enough for us to know that Paul had a prayer request, apparently something he wanted removed because it weakened him. Then Paul learned that in his weakness God's strength was made perfect. The person who will not admit to any weakness is a person who is living entirely off his own strength. He cannot find God's strength perfected in him because the Lord's strength is perfected through the acknowledgement of a weakness. Subsequently he is in bondage to his own fallible words and actions. He doesn't have faith in God. At best, he has faith in his own faith.

God is our strength. If we boast in anything, we are to boast in the Lord. As I struggled with my weakness, I didn't fully understand what God was doing in my life, so I asked Him one day, "Lord, how long will I have to live with this temptation?" He answered, "Ron, temptation is not sin. To have a weakness is not sin. Only yielding to either of them is sin. But remember that with temptation, I will always provide a way out." This is corroborated by Scripture.

> *No temptation has overtaken you but such as is common to man; and God is faithful, who will not allow you to be tempted beyond what you are able, but with the temptation will provide the way of escape also, that you may be able to endure it (1 Cor. 10:13).*

Weakness is meant to draw us to God. So when I am tempted, if I will draw on God's strength by spending time in prayer, then I have an opportunity to become strong in the Lord through my weakness. God's people have always seized upon this opportunity. Moses did in Exodus 17. As a battle raged, the Hebrews won so long as Moses sat on a hill with his hands raised to God, which was a sign of surrender. I have always found it interesting to contemplate what the leader of the enemy army thought as he and his men charged forth and saw the ancient Hebrew leader sitting on a hill in a position of surrender. He must have thought, "This is going to be easy. Their leader has already surrendered." But as long as Moses was in that position of surrender, the Hebrews were invincible. Only when Moses dropped his hands, which was symbolic of trying to fight the battle in human strength, did God's people begin to lose.

We all need to allow God to develop His strength through our weaknesses. I don't just sit back and say, "Praise God! I'm weak!" That misses the point. The key is not that I'm weak, but that I can say, "God, I'm weak and **I need You.**"

That acknowledgement brought me to the place where I really began to seek God, not just things from Him.

This is where our free will becomes the greatest gift that God has given us. I can choose to stick with God and pray until I have victory over it. I could also choose to give up and consider my weakness too overwhelming to be reckoned with. With my weakness, I chose to pray through it, and that freedom of choice has become the source of God's greatest blessings in my life. You have the same freedom of choice where your marriage is concerned. You can either decide to stick with it (and with God) or you can choose to give up. IF you choose God's way, that choice will become a source of great blessing to you.

The Third Example: The Letter to the Hebrews

> *Therefore, do not throw away your confidence, which has a great reward. For you have need of endurance, so that when you have done the will of God, you may received what was promised. For yet in a very little while, He who is coming will come, and will not delay. But My righteous one shall live by faith; and if he shrinks back, My soul has pleasure in him (Heb. 10:35-38).*

Verse 35 admonishes us not to throw away our faith and to expect a great reward for continuing to believe God. The reason it tells us not to throw away our faith is because that's when we need it most. Our prayer request is not yet about to be granted and that's when our faith in God is tested. Your faith in God will enable you to continue to pray even though you don't see the answer you would like to at that particular moment. If God tells us to continue to pray, the faith it takes to continue to pray will ultimately bring you to the place where you have faith for the answer. I have witnessed this time and time again. At one point, I had been praying about a certain matter for many weeks. One night as I was praying about it, I sensed the Lord saying, "Ron, you no longer need to pray about this situation. Consider it resolved even though you do not see the resolution right now." Because I had prayed so long about it, the next day I thought I would just remind Him of the answer He promised me. As soon as I began praying about it, I sense the Holy Spirit saying, "Ron, I dealt with you about that already. To continue to pray about it now would be a lack of faith." God can bring us to the place where we can practice Romans 4:17, where we can call things that are not as though they were. However, it does require faith. It takes faith to pray about something that has not yet happened, and it takes faith to stop praying when God tells you to.

Our faith pays us great dividends. There is great recompense of reward with our faith, but it isn't just a matter of trying to muster great faith on our own. Our ability to continue to pray is a sign of faith. While we are in prayer, God continues to make us into that person He wants us to be. That is why the writer of Hebrews says in verse 36, "For you have need of endurance [patience]." Right after telling us not to give up our faith, he says, "You need patience." As we have already determined, the development of patience in our lives is God shaping us into the kind of person He wants us to be. The reason the prayer is not answered yet is that God is still working in the life of the pray-er. You have need of patience.

If you understand that God is endeavoring to make you into the person He wants you to be and that through that development your prayer will be answered, you should strive to become all that God wants you to be. You should set your life on a course of following God's will. The writer of Hebrews assumes we understand this as he states in the last part of verse 36, "...so that when you have done the will of God [when you have become the person He wants you to be], you may receive what was promised." The prayer is answered!

Verse 38 says it a third time, "But My righteous one shall live by faith...." Right after telling us to continue to pray, it talks about faith. God is bringing us to a point where He can work through us. That is why there are times when a prayer is simply not going to be answered until God has the opportunity to shape us. That's why no matter how much faith you try to exercise, there are times when God will not answer a certain prayer until He has shaped you. God is more concerned with who the pray-er is than the answer to the prayer. Some situations take much prayer, others don't.

Some people are quick to point to John 15:7 which says, "If you abide in Me, and My words abide in you, ask whatever you wish, and it shall be done for you." Using this verse as a basis, they postulate that one can and should receive rewards for faith unconditionally. There is a condition though: we must abide in Him. In 1 John 2:6, we find the conditions for abiding: "The one who says he abides in Him ought himself to walk in the same manner as He walked." That's the only way we can claim John 15:7. We must be like Christ, and that is who God is making us like in prayer. He draws us to prayer by using our weaknesses. By drawing us to Him through our weakness, His strength is perfected in us. He brings us to a place of faith, and through that faith, our prayers are answered. Our time of prayer is meant to develop such a relationship with God that even after He answers our prayers, we will keep praying. Then your prayer time begins to direct your whole life, and God begins to do great things through what He has developed in you.

CHAPTER NINETEEN

Keeping The Vow

When you make a vow to God, do not be late in paying it, for He takes no delight in fools. Pay what you vow! (Eccles. 5:4).

For the most part, people in our world do not esteem a vow to be of much value. There was a time just a century ago when business agreements could be sealed by a handshake. A man's honor was considered to be an insoluble bond that would cement a deal. Today, we require a written contract for almost any agreement. Then many will attempt to violate the spirit of the contract by finding a loophole which will permit them to do so, and often the matter will end up in court. Living in such a culture, it is imperative that we understand how God feels about vows. To God, vows are a sacred thing.

It is a snare for a man to say rashly, "It is holy!" And after the vows to make inquiry (Prov. 20:25).

Obviously, a snare is a trap. Apparently, so is a broken vow. If you make a vow rashly, and then try to get out of it, you will be trapped. To question what you have done after it is done is where the problem lies. A vow becomes a holy statement, and holiness is a great part of God's character. It is a very serious matter.

I recall speaking to a particular man who was going through a divorce because his wife had left him. I asked him if he knew if his wife had even given consideration to the vows she had taken at their wedding ceremony. He said he knew exactly what she thought about those vows because he had asked her. She said, "I didn't pay any attention to what I said. Those vows didn't mean a thing. They were just empty words."

Did you know that the Church cannot marry you to someone? Your pastor cannot even marry you to someone. Do you know what marries you? It's your vow. During the ceremony, the pastor asks a series of questions to the effect, "Do you take this woman/man to be your lawfully wedded wife/husband? Do you solemnly promise before God and these witnesses to love, honor, and cherish him/her in sickness and in health, for richer or poorer, to have and to hold until death do you part?" The moment you answer, "I do," you are married in God's sight because you made that vow. That statement binds you to your mate. Trying to get out of that vow traps you. You are trapped the rest of your life because of the words of your mouth. Even if you get a divorce, you will always feel the effects of that broken vow.

Samson: An Object Lesson On Broken Vows

I once heard Morris Williams, a missionary, discuss Samson with special attention to his broken vow. He had taken the vow to be a Nazarite, a vow dedicating himself to the Lord. It consisted of three parts: (1) a vow to abstain from strong drink (Num. 6:3); (2) a vow to abstain from haircuts (Num. 6:5); and (3) a vow to abstain from touching any dead body (Num. 6:6). The vow concluded, "All the days of his separation he is holy to the Lord" (Num. 6:8). What made his separation holy? The fulfillment of his vow.

Samson's story really began when, as a young man, he chose a wife who lived in the valley of Timnah, literally, "the valley of the grape" (Judg. 14:1). This was his first mistake because his vow to abstain from strong drink also included fresh and dried grapes. Nonetheless, he went to see her, but on his way, a lion leaped out at him. With his amazing strength, Samson killed the lion with his bare hands. Samson found that even as he was on his way to break his vow, the Spirit of the Lord was still upon him and he was able to kill the lion with ease.

Just about that time, Samson began asking himself the same question many Christians are asking themselves today: How far can I go? Today believers are preoccupied with questions like, "What can we do and still be saved?" and "How many worldly activities can we involve ourselves in and still be saved?" Just as we make a vow to serve the Lord at the moment of salvation, Samson made a vow to the Lord. Like many of God's people today, he wanted to know how much he could get away with and still have his strength. It became apparent that his flirtation with the grapes hadn't resulted in the loss of any of his strength. At that moment, he began playing with sin, figuring he could do so with impunity (exempt from punishment).

When he returned home, he noticed there was something different about the dead lion. "...He turned aside to look at the carcass of the lion; and behold, a swarm of bees and honey were in the body of the lion" (Judg. 14:8). Samson, not so hygiene-conscious as modern Americans, was tempted by the sight of the honey. His vow strictly prohibited touching a dead body of any kind, though. To us, the dead lion is symbolic of all that we put to death when we made our respective vows to live for God, giving up our past lives. We repented of certain things and vowed to have nothing to do with them, much like Samson. He found himself confronted with his past life, and he found that what he had put to death was enticing him. Judges 14:9 records the choice he made: "So he scraped the honey into his hands and went on...." In the process, he undoubtedly touched the dead carcass.

Samson had broken two parts of his Nazarite vow and yet he found that he had not lost his strength. He was still able to kill one thousand men single-handedly. Playing with sin still seemed like a safe pastime for Samson. Then he met Delilah. She was a type of Satan, depicting the presence and persistence of Satan that comes into our lives or our marriages when we begin to back off from our vows. Delilah was not very subtle in her attempts to trap Samson. She said, "Please tell me where your great strength is and how you may be bound to afflict you." She was very obvious. Samson could not possibly have been deceived by her. He knew what her game was, but arrogantly thought she was no threat to him. He gave her false answers for a while. He told her he would be powerless if he was bound with ropes that had never been used before. She bound him with such ropes, and he broke them like strings, but Samson still saw no threat. When she saw he was still strong, Samson told her he would really be like any other man if he was bound with fresh branches, but in the end, he was still strong. He was still playing with sin and still saw no threat. So he went even further. He told her, "If you weave the seven lock of my hair...then I shall become weak...."

This was an important step. His playing with sin had weakened his resistance. His answers to Delilah were getting closer to the truth. He didn't want her to cut his hair, yet he was allowing her to braid it. When that failed to achieve the results Delilah had been seeking, she continued pressuring him until he broke down and told her, "A razor has never come on my head...." With that, Samson had broken every one of his vows, and his strength was gone. His strength was not in his hair, but in his vow. "And he awoke from his sleep...[he thought he was strong]. But he did not know that the Lord had departed from him."

Samson played with sin and got caught. The same is true of many Christians today, but most often, we blame it on Satan. There has been much discussion about how Satan is attacking the family unit. I don't believe we are in the midst of a satanic attack as much as we are in the mist of worldly lust. Christian families have been submerging themselves in worldly activities and have emerged with humanistic

thoughts. Then they've blamed their collapsing family struc-
tures on Satan. The problem we have today is that we have
been experimenting with worldly activities and have come to
the conclusion that it's okay. Like Samson, we don't think
we're going to get burned if we play with fire. Furthermore,
like Samson, we keep going further and further. We indulge
in one form of worldly activity and then jump right into
another. Then when we see we're still saved, we head for yet
another. We claim we're not harmed by it. But what consti-
tutes harm? Is not an exploding divorce rate within the
Church harm enough? Are not broken families and shattered
lives harm enough?

Regardless of whether or not you admit it, the strength
of you relationship with God lies in your adherence to your
vow to Him. That's called holiness. Without it, you can still be
a Christian, but you cannot have a strong relationship with
God. You may want to keep your lifestyle, but if you do and
neglect holiness, you will have to face the terrible consequences of your actions just as Samson did. Galatians 5:4
states, "You have been severed from Christ, you who are
seeking to be justified by the law; you have fallen from grace."
So, friend, if you have made a vow, pray daily that you will
keep it. Don't play with sin.

There was some good news about Samson. In the end, he
repented and regained his strength. Then in one great effort,
he accomplished more for God than all his other feats com-
bined had. If you have gone back on your vow to live for God,
you can still ask God to forgive you and start drawing from
His strength through daily prayer.

New Release!

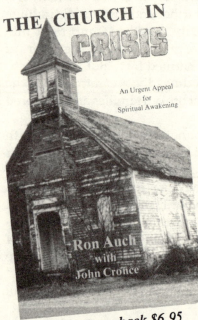

THE CHURCH IN

CRISIS

An Urgent Appeal
for
Spiritual Awakening

Ron Auch
with
John Cronce

Trade Paperback $6.95

THE CHURCH IN CRISIS

by Ron Auch

The church of Jesus Christ in America is in great need of a revival.

In this book the author looks at the role prayer has played and will play in reviving the Church. Without a powerful move of God, our nation has no hope.

"To me, a book is worthy of the designation 'classic' when it not only has the potential to impact generations to come, but when it includes a clear message from God that speaks with uncompromising authority to any who take time to read it. *Church In Crisis* clearly meets those qualifications. Ron Auch has most certainly heard from the Lord on the Church's desperate need for awakening." *Dick Eastman — Every Home For Christ*

ISBN: 0-89221-181-4

New Leaf 🕊 Press

P.O. BOX 311 • GREEN FOREST, AR 72638
1-800-643-9535